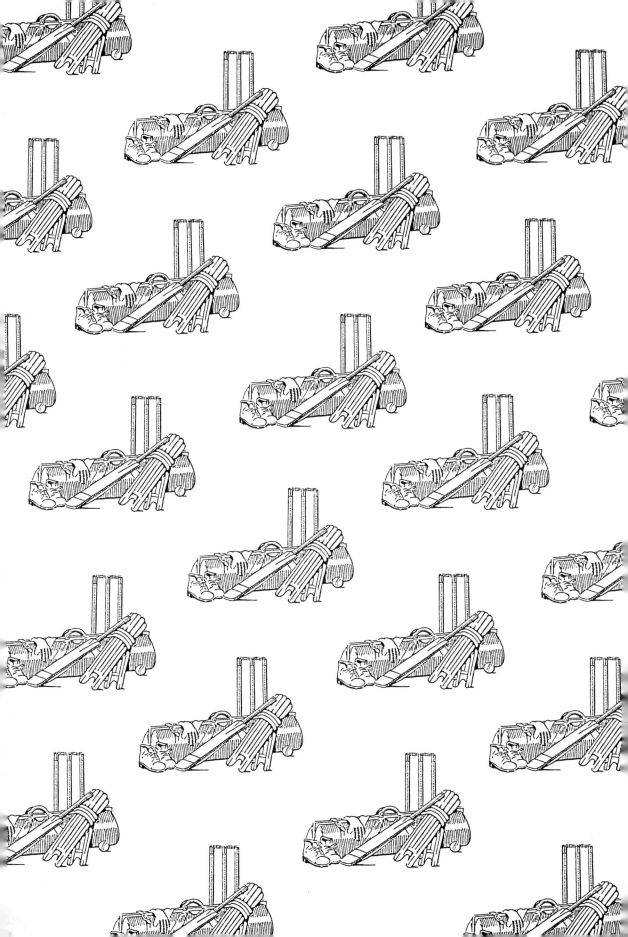

THE CRICKETER BOOK
of CRICKET DAYS

COMPILED BY *Chris Rhys*

GENERAL
EDITOR *Christopher Martin-Jenkins*

Queen Anne Press

A QUEEN ANNE PRESS BOOK

© Lennard Associates Ltd 1993

This paperback edition published in 1993 by
Queen Anne Press, a division of
Lennard Associates Ltd
Mackerye End
Harpenden, Herts AL5 5DR

First published in 1989 by Lennard Publishing

A catalogue entry is available from the British Library

ISBN 1 85291 537 4

Edited by Michael Leitch
Designed by Cooper Wilson
Typesetting by Goodfellow and Egan, Cambridge

Printed and bound in England by
The Bath Press, Bath, Avon.

CONTENTS

INTRODUCTION

Cricket is the most sociable of sports. There must be more cricket dinners round the world every year than there are for all other sports put together, although Rugby no doubt occupies second place.

It is a convention that such dinners should have speeches when the coffee cups have been cleared away (or sometimes whilst they are being cleared away, one of many hazards facing the inexperienced speaker). Occasionally one hears Members of Parliament cast in the role of after-dinner entertainer and I have noticed that all of them have certain things in common. They insist on speaking first; they can never resist making a party point or two; and they always leave immediately after their speech, if possible to a standing ovation, claiming that they have to go to Westminster to vote.

If this is just a ploy to avoid hearing two more speeches, including some familiar stories, not to mention the auction, followed by an ear-bashing from anyone in the room politically enough minded to cross-examine them about various topical matters, I don't blame them for using it. In some cases, perhaps, it is merely a good excuse for an early night, or even for a late one with the secretary!

Usually, and not surprisingly, these MPs are very good speakers and I have also noticed that more than one of them uses a technique of recalling some significant or amusing event which happened many years ago on the date in question, often a useful peg on which to hang a speech. I have tried to find a suitable book of days to aid my own occasional visits to the podium – in vain, until now.

This collection will be, I hope, a boon for anyone called to 'say a few words' at a cricket dinner, whether it be at Little Peover C.C. (a genuine club in Cheshire by the way and pronounced 'Pee-ver', in case you wondered) or before 1000 people at the Forty Club in a Park Lane hotel in London.

Cricket has a long history and the research of Chris Rhys has produced something of significance for every day of the year, with much else left out. The Test début of Jack Hobbs on the first day of January 1908 is not a bad start, and on the same day 17 years later Bill Ponsford scored the second Test hundred of a career which began in a blaze of glory and continued in prolific vein, even if it was eventually upstaged by the Don.

One thing leads to another when you begin dealing with cricket dates. I had not realised before that on my birthday Mushtaq Mohammad made 303 not out for the Karachi Blues (I would have bought him a drink but he is a devout Moslem!) or that on the same date Billy Bates of Nottinghamshire had taken the first hat-trick for England – a useful one, too: McDonnell, Giffen and Bonnor.

My wife, though she does not fully appreciate the fact, shares a birthday with three redoubtable England cricketers, and characters all: Brian Close, Derek Randall and John Lever. She also shares with them a sense of humour and great loyalty but I wouldn't want to go too far, as astrologers might, and suggest too many comparisons: for example she bats right-handed on the beach and, touch wood, shows no sign of baldness!

Our wedding anniversary coincides with the death of J.T. Hearne, whose lively but alas unfinished diary of his tour of Australia we once published in *The Cricketer* and who lived to the respectable age of 76 despite a long and hard-working cricket career in which he took over 3000 first-class wickets, bowling more then 10,000 balls in 1896. Six winters spent coaching and playing in India for the Maharajah of Patiala also suggests a strong constitution.

So one could go on: one of my brothers has a birthday on the anniversary of the start of the highest county Championship score, Yorkshire's indulgent 887 against Warwickshire, and on the same date Duleepsinhji made 333 for Sussex against Northamptonshire at Hove. Perhaps one of my sons will equal the feat: one was born on the same day as another prolific Sussex player (though only briefly so), Javed Miandad; the other first saw the light on the anniversary of a day on which four Australian Test batsmen, Jack Gregory, Tommy Andrews, Alan Kippax and Archie Jackson all made hundreds for New South Wales against the touring New Zealanders. Not to be outdone, my daughter was born exactly 49 years after Don Bradman's immortal 309 not out at Headingley on July 11th 1930.

Most of us can hum the tune of the song 'This is my lucky Day'. Maybe Sir Donald will recall that hot day in Leeds on the day he dies. Certainly many who saw him displaying his God-given gifts to the full that day will have remembered the occasion many times since. Whether there is such a thing as a lucky *date* for cricketers, however, is less likely than the undoubted fact that players have lucky grounds. I recently read Derek Underwood, for example, recalling some of the marvellous things which happened to him whenever he played cricket at the Priory ground at Hastings. Nevertheless one wonders if it was just coincidence that V.E. Walker, one of the famous Southgate family, took all 10 wickets twice in his career, both times on July 22nd? V.E. Day indeed!

One the first occasion, in 1859, his figures of 10 for 74 were achieved for 'England' against Surrey: aged only 22 then, he took four for 17 in the second innings with his lobs, having also scored 20 not out and 108. It is customary, by the way, to talk of the 'famous Southgate Walkers'. Like the Fosters of Worcestershire there were seven of them, but one of my favourite footnotes in *Scores and Biographies* is this one:

Mr. W.H. Walker is not one of the famous Walker family of Southgate.

Poor old W.H. I am not quite sure when he was born; probably February 29th!

Christopher Martin-Jenkins

JANUARY

1

1908   Jack Hobbs makes his Test début against Australia at the Melbourne Cricket Ground. His innings of 83 and 28 help England to victory by one wicket.

1923   Two notable débuts enliven the second Test at Cape Town during England's tour of South Africa. G.G. Macauley (England) dismisses G.A.L. Hearne with his first ball in Test cricket, and makes the winning hit in England's one-wicket victory. For South Africa, débutant pace bowler A.E. Hall turns in figures of 4 for 49 and 7 for 63, giving him a match analysis of 62.3–20–112–11.

1925   W.H. Ponsford (Australia) becomes the first to score a century in each of his first two Test matches. Following his 128, Australia win the second Test at Melbourne by 81 runs.

1967   Maurice Leyland dies at the age of 66. He made his début for Yorkshire in 1920 and stayed with the county as coach from 1951 to 1963. He put on a record 2nd-wicket partnership of 382 with Len Hutton at the Oval in 1938. In first-class cricket he scored 33,660 runs at 40.50 and took 466 wickets at 29.31.

WILLS'S CIGARETTES

M. LEYLAND

Wills for Quality
CRICKETERS
2ND SERIES OF 50

26
M. Leyland.
(Yorkshire.)

Son of a good bowler, Maurice Leyland became professional to the Harrogate Club, and graded into the Yorkshire eleven in 1921. Coming of age during that summer he consolidated his position two seasons later, and gradually matured, until last year, by scoring 1,783—average 54, highest innings 247 —he ripened into an England cricketer. With 102 in the Test Trial at Lord's in 1927 he showed the right temperament, while brilliant fielding in the deep and slow bowling make this all-round left-hander the ideal type for touring Australia after coaching in India.

W.D.& H.O. WILLS
ISSUED BY THE IMPERIAL TOBACCO CO.
(OF GREAT BRITAIN & IRELAND) LTD

2

1879   F.A. Mackinnon makes his Test début for England against Australia. Full name The Mackinnon of Mackinnon, 35th Chief of the Clan of Mackinnon, he possesses one of the longest titles in cricket but is the second victim in a Spofforth hat-trick and this proves to be his only Test appearance. Spofforth's feat is the first hat-trick in Test match history. His other victims are V.P.F.A. Royle and T. Emmett. Also making his Test début in this match is A.N. Hornby, one of only two players to captain England at both cricket and Rugby Union.

1973   John Benaud, brother of Richie, makes 142 for Australia v Pakistan at Melbourne in the second Test, scoring 93 before lunch. Before going in to bat he is informed that he will be dropped for the next Test!

1979   On the fourth day of the third Test between India and West Indies at Eden Gardens, Calcutta, Sunil Gavaskar reaches his second century of the match. This is the third time he has scored a century in each innings of a Test match.

1985   Clive Lloyd ends his great run as captain of West Indies in a record 74 Tests. This match also ends the finest undefeated run of a Test captain: after 27 matches, the first of which was in December 1981, his team lose to Australia by an innings and 85 runs.

3

1886   Birth of Arthur Mailey, Australian leg-break and googly bowler, part-time recluse, reporter, cartoonist and, on his retirement from cricket, butcher, having a placard outside his shop which says, after his name, 'used to bowl tripe, used to write tripe, now he sells

The Nawab of Pataudi features on the front of a programme for the 1967 Indian tour.

Clive Lloyd with Viv Richards, his successor as West Indies captain.

tripe'. In his first-class career Mailey takes 779 wickets at 24.10 and 99 Test wickets at 33.91.

1939   Don Tallon of Queensland equals Edward Pooley's 70-year-old record for most dismissals in a match: against New South Wales at Sydney he catches nine and stumps three.

1949   Everton Weekes completes a record run, still unequalled, of five successive Test centuries. In the third Test v India at Calcutta he scores 162 in the first innings and 101 in the second to set the record.

4

1898   E. Jones (Australia) becomes the first player to be no-balled in a Test match. The opponents are England, the umpire is J. Phillips, the venue Melbourne.

1902   Australia beat England by 229 runs in the second Test at Melbourne. The match ends with Hugh Trumble dismissing Jones, Gunn and Barnes in successive balls.

1929   Don Bradman scores his first Test century – 112 in the third Test against England at Melbourne.

1949   Denis Compton takes 5 for 70 v South Africa in the third Test at Cape Town – his only five-wicket haul in Test cricket.

5

1904   Wilfred Rhodes completes his dismissal of 15 Australian batsmen (7–56, 8–68) in the second Test at Melbourne.

1941   Birth of Mansur Ali Khan Pataudi (Nawab of Pataudi, jnr). Like his father he is to captain India, and in 1962 at the age of 21 he becomes the youngest-ever Test captain.

1971   Australia meet England in the first one-day international, arranged after rain ruins the Test match; Australia win by 5 wickets.

1983   Zaheer Abbas (Pakistan), with 168 against India at Faisalabad, makes his third successive Test score of more than 150.

JANUARY

6

1891 Birth of Ted McDonald in Tasmania. After 11 Test appearances for Australia, opening the bowling in a successful and widely feared partnership with Jack Gregory, he moves to England and qualifies for Lancashire.

1930 Don Bradman passes Ponsford's world-record score of 437 and goes on to make 452* for New South Wales v Queensland at Sydney.

1959 Birth of Kapil Dev. The Indian all-rounder begins his Test career at the age of 19 and in 1983 captains his country to World Cup glory.

7

1930 Following Bradman's 452*, New South Wales beat Queensland by the record margin of 685 runs.

1956 Vinoo Mankad (231) and Pankaj Roy (173) put on 413 for India's first wicket v New Zealand in Madras, a world record in Test cricket. The previous record: 359 by Len Hutton and Cyril Washbrook for England v South Africa in Johannesburg, 1948–49.

1987 Kapil Dev becomes the second player after Ian Botham to score 3,000 runs and take 300 Test wickets when he dismisses Ravi Ratnayeke (Sri Lanka) in the third Test at Cuttack.

8

1863 Formation of present Yorkshire CCC.

1923 Birth at Ardsley of John Wardle, controversial slow left-armer for Yorkshire and England. In 28 Tests he

takes 102 wickets at only 20.39. After making criticisms in the Press of the Yorkshire captain, he is left out of the county side.

1949 Birth of Lawrence Rowe in Kingston, Jamaica. On his Test début he scores a century and a double century, and in a later Test he hits a triple century.

9

1871 Birth of C.J. Kortright, the fastest bowler of his era, at Ingatestone, Essex. Between 1895 and 1898 his 297 wickets include 201 clean-bowled.

1911 South Africa complete a first innings total of 482 against Australia. This

Vinoo Mankad joins George Headley to open the innings for a Commonwealth XI against an England XI at the Kingston Cricket Festival in 1951.

forms the base of the largest Test aggregate (at that time) of 1646 (for 40 wickets). South Africa (482 and 360) beat Australia (465 and 339) by 38 runs.

1971   Bob Willis, future England captain, makes his Test début at Melbourne in the third Test – before he has been awarded his county cap.

10

1911   Victor Trumper (Australia) hits 200 in 226 minutes against South Africa, a new record for the fastest Test double century.

1930   Maurice Allom makes his Test début in the first ever Test match against New Zealand and takes four wickets in five balls, including a hat-trick.

1977   Rodney Marsh completes a rare double for Western Australia v South Australia, scoring 104 and taking 10 catches in the match.

1988   Uproar over bonus payments in South Africa. Clive Rice opts to bat on and Transvaal amass 587–8 dec, with Jimmy Cook (150), Bruce Roberts (174) and Rice (150*) all picking up R10,000 bonuses for scoring 150. Next day Piet Visagie scores 164 for Northern Transvaal. The bonus payouts amount to more than the prize-money for winning the Currie Cup.

11

1827   Formation of the original Norfolk CCC.

1930   J.E.D. Sealy makes his début for West Indies v England at Bridgetown at the age of 17 years 121 days – still a West Indian record. Also making their Test débuts in this match are George Headley (West Indies) and Bill Voce (England).

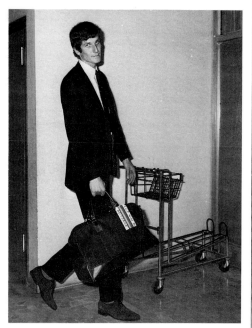

Bob Willis leaves London on his first England tour.

1959   Hanif Mohammad completes his world-record first-class score of 499 for Karachi v Bahawalpur, made in 635 minutes. Going for 500, he is run out off the last ball of the day.

12

1864   Formation of Lancashire CCC.

1940   Birth of New Zealand Test cricketer Dick Motz in Christchurch. At one time holder of the world record for most runs scored in an over in Test cricket (22), he also becomes the first New Zealander to take 100 Test wickets.

1960   Gary Sobers (226 with 24 fours in 647 minutes) and Frank Worrell (197* with two sixes and 17 fours in 682 minutes) save the first Test for West Indies v England at Bridgetown and set a record for the highest-ever Test stand in West Indies Test cricket (399 runs).

JANUARY

13

1832 Death of Thomas Lord, founder of Lord's Cricket Ground and in his playing days a competent slow underarm bowler.

1930 England play in two Test matches on the same day – against New Zealand at Christchurch and against West Indies at Bridgetown. This is the only instance in Test history.

1933 'Bodyline' tactics break out for the first time in Test cricket when Harold Larwood and Bill Voce bowl leg theory to the Australians in the third Test at Adelaide. Bill Woodfull is battered by bouncers and Bertie Oldfield deflects a ball into his face.

14

1876 Formation of present Essex CCC, who must wait 103 years before winning their first major trophies, the 1979 County Championship and the Benson & Hedges Cup.

1898 Joe Darling hits the first-ever six in Test cricket without the aid of overthrows. The ball goes out of the Adelaide ground as Darling reaches his century; he goes on to make 178.

1964 R.G. Nadkarni completes the remarkable analysis of 32–27–5–0 including 21 successive maidens in the first Test v England at Madras.

15

1895 Albert Trott (Australia) celebrates his Test début by taking eight English wickets for 43 at Adelaide.

1963 John Murray takes 100 minutes to score three runs for England v Australia at Sydney.

Harold Larwood and Bill Voce get together again at Trent Bridge in 1977.

England's impressive total at Madras.

1985 Graeme Fowler (201) and Mike Gatting (207) become the first pair of English batsmen each to score a double century in the same Test innings, v India at Madras.

1988 India's Narendra Hirwani completes match figures of 16–136 on his Test début v West Indies, the third-best all-time figures in Test cricket after Jim Laker (19–90 in 1956) and Sydney Barnes (17–159 in 1913–14).

16

1895 R. Slade Lucas leads the first English team to tour the West Indies. His side win 10, draw 3, lose 4.

1933 Death of Archie Jackson (Australia). Two years before, Jackson had TB, then in 1932 he began playing club cricket against doctors' orders.

1956 Birth of Wayne Daniel, marvellous servant of Middlesex cricket, in St Phillip, Barbados.

17

1931 Don Bradman completes his innings of 223 against the West Indies at Brisbane to record the highest score (at that time) by an Australian in a home Test.

1958 Nasim-ul-Ghani makes his Test début for Pakistan v West Indies at Bridgetown. At the age of 16 years 248 days he becomes the youngest-ever Test player. Also making his Test début in this match is Haseeb Ahsan, in 1987 the controversial team manager on Pakistan's tour to England.

1985 England amass 652 for 7 dec v India at Madras. Victory in this match gives them the series 2–1.

JANUARY

1933   At 3.12 pm the Australian Cricket Board vote 8–5 to send a cable to the MCC in London 'deploring the use of Bodyline'.

1939   In his sixth innings of the 1938–39 season Don Bradman scores his sixth successive century, equalling C.B. Fry's record established in 1901.

1978   Test début of Mike Gatting v Pakistan in the third Test at Karachi.

1922   Birth of Australia's opening bat in 46 Tests, Arthur Morris. The left-hander scores 3,533 Test runs at 46.48 and averages 53.67 in first-class matches.

1930   Birth of John Waite, South Africa's most-capped player. In 50 Tests the wicket-keeper/batsman scores 2,405 runs at 30.44 and makes 141 dismissals.

1933   Last day of infamous third Test between Australia and England at

Adelaide. Larwood (4–71) and Voce (4–50) bowl out Australia for 193 and England win by 338 runs.

2 0

1883 W. Bates takes the first England hat-trick in a Test, dismissing P.S. McDonnell (3), G. Giffen (0) and G.J. Bonnor (0) for an analysis of 26.2–14–28–7.

1895 Birth of famous umpire Frank Chester at Bushey, Herts. After losing a hand in the First World War he becomes a first-class umpire at the age of 27 and stands in a record 48 Test matches between 1924 and 1955.

1967 Test début of Mike Procter, one of the world's foremost all-rounders, for South Africa v Australia at Durban. Because of *apartheid* he is to play in only seven Tests.

1968 Mushtaq Mohammad makes his highest score – 303* for Karachi Blues v Karachi University.

The young Mike Gatting, fifth from the left, stands between Bob Taylor and Ken Barrington with the England team to tour Pakistan and New Zealand in 1978.

An awkward moment for South African wicket-keeper John Waite at Trent Bridge in 1955.

JANUARY

21

1954   George Headley plays his 22nd and final Test match for West Indies, v England at Kingston. Then aged 44 years 236 days he remains the oldest cricketer to represent West Indies.

1956   England Test captain M.J.K. Smith plays Rugby Union for England v Wales at Twickenham. Wales win 8–3 and that is the end of Smith's career as a Rugby international!

1964   Test début of great Indian spinner Bagwhat Chandrasekhar v England in Bombay. His figures: 40–16–67–4.

22

1902   Clem Hill fails to reach his Test century for the third time in a row, bowled by Jessop for 97; in the first innings he scored 98 and in the second innings of the previous Test he reached 99.

1948   Twelve players make their Test débuts in the West Indies v England match at Bridgetown including Everton Weekes, Clyde Walcott and Jim Laker who takes 7 for 103 in the first innings.

1970   Barry Richards makes his Test début for South Africa in their last official series, v Australia. He scores 508 runs at 72.57 and on that high note his Test career comes to an end.

23

1948   Don Bradman passes 200 in a Test for the twelfth and final time, v India at Adelaide.

1958   Hanif Mohammad scores 337 for Pakistan v West Indies at Bridgetown. It takes him 970 minutes – the longest innings in first-class cricket – and saves the match.

1971   At the Commonwealth Prime Ministers' Conference in Singapore a communiqué is issued which forms the basis of the Gleneagles Agreement, drawn up in 1977.

24

1930   J.E. Mills (117) scores the first début Test century for New Zealand, sharing an opening stand of 276 with C.S. Dempster (136) v England at Wellington.

1962   Another Test marathon by Hanif Mohammad (see 23rd). Against England at Dacca he scores 104 in 393 minutes in the second innings after scoring 111 in 500 minutes in the first, thereby occupying the crease for almost 15 hours.

1983   Mudassar Nazar (152*) carries his bat through the Pakistan innings v India at Lahore. In 1952 his father, Nazar Mohammad, did the same, scoring 124* in Pakistan's first-ever Test win and becoming the first man to remain on the field throughout a Test match.

1956 CRICKETERS
A SERIES OF FIFTY
(1st SERIES, NUMBERS 1 to 25)

No. 14
BRIAN STATHAM
(Lancashire and England)
England's greatest bowling victory over the 1955 South African touring team was when Manchester-born Brian Statham took 7 for 39 at Lord's in a non-stop spell of 3 hours and 10 minutes. A 26-year-old left-hand bat and accurate right-arm fast bowler, he took 84 wickets at an average of 12.82 in 1955 in championship matches.

Distributed by CBT LONDON W.2
ISSUED BY KANE PRODUCTS LTD.

25

1910 N.C. Tufnell (England), replacing Herbert Strudwick, achieves the first Test stumping by a substitute as he dismisses S.J. Snooke (53) v South Africa at Durban.

1952 Richie Benaud, first man to the Test double of 2,000 runs and 200 wickets, makes his début for Australia v West Indies at Sydney.

1963 Brian Statham breaks Alec Bedser's world record of 236 Test wickets in the fourth Test v Australia at Adelaide.

1976 Surinder Amarnath achieves a unique family double by scoring a century (124) on his Test début v New Zealand at Auckland. In 1933 his father Lala scored 118 on his first appearance for India in the country's first home Test, v England at Bombay.

26

1878 Birth of Arthur 'Dave' Nourse, South Africa's finest captain in their early Test years, in Croydon, Surrey. He emigrates to South Africa at the age of 17 and represents them 45 times in 22 years.

1906 Victor Trumper hits 101 out of 139 for New South Wales v Victoria at Sydney, reaching his century in 57 minutes.

1954 Birth of Kim Hughes at Margaret River, Western Australia. Though a fine player, he suffers from adverse publicity while captaining Australia and breaks down in tears at a Press conference.

Dave Nourse bowling against Leicestershire in 1924.

Troubled times for Australian captain Kim Hughes.

JANUARY

27

1887 England are bowled out for 45 by Australia in the first Test at Sydney (C.T.B. Turner 6 for 15 on his début). England fight back through Barnes and Lohmann and win by 13 runs.

1912 Frank Woolley hits 305* for MCC v Tasmania at Hobart, including three sixes and 43 fours.

1964 Eddie Barlow (201) and Graeme Pollock (175) complete their stand of 341 for South Africa v Australia at Adelaide – a South African Test record for all wickets.

1981 England bowler Robin Jackman is served with a deportation order by the Guyanese Government when England arrive to play a Test against the West Indies. Jackman, whose wife is South African, played cricket for several seasons in the Republic.

28

1935 Learie Constantine (14.5–9–11–3) is warned for repeated use of the short-pitched delivery as West Indies bowl England out for 107 to win the second Test at Port of Spain by 217 runs.

1949 Everton Weekes (West Indies) with five successive centuries in Test matches under his belt, is run out for 90 in the fourth Test v India at Madras.

1965 Death of A.P. 'Tich' Freeman at the age of 76, the only man to take 300 wickets in a season (304 in 1928). He reached 100 wickets 17 times and 200 a record eight times. He took 3,776 first-class wickets at 18.42 with a best analysis of 10–53.

29

1957 Hugh Tayfield bowls 137 balls without conceding a run for South Africa v England at Durban. He completes 16 eight-ball maidens and finishes with figures of 37.7–14–69–8.

1969 Ian Redpath (Australia) is run out by Charlie Griffith (West Indies) for backing up too far in the fourth Test at Adelaide. Australia, needing 359 to win, are 339 for 9 at the end.

1971 Dennis Lillee (Australia), soon to become the world's finest fast bowler, makes his Test début in the sixth Test v England at Adelaide.

Dennis Lillee on his Test début in 1971.

30

1929 Birth in Durban of Hugh Tayfield, South Africa's record Test wicket-taker. He holds his country's records for most Test wickets (170), best bowling (9 for 113) and best match aggregate (13 for 156).

1961 West Indian off-spinner Lance Gibbs completes a Test hat-trick v Australia at Adelaide, dismissing Mackay, Grout and Mission.

1988 England opener Chris Broad is fined £500 for smashing a stump after being bowled by Steve Waugh in the Bicentennial Test at Sydney.

31

1933 The British Cabinet are consulted over the problem of the Australian Cricket Board's cable in the Bodyline dispute.

1944 Birth of John Inverarity (Western Australia), the leading scorer in Sheffield Shield history.

1976 Lance Gibbs takes the world record for Test dismissals when he has Redpath caught by Holding in the sixth Test at Adelaide. Redpath becomes his 308th victim. Later the same day he takes his last Test wicket, that of Gilmour.

JANUARY

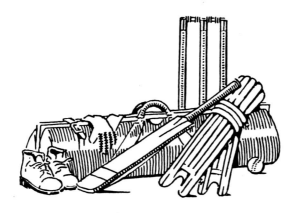

FEBRUARY

1

1930 Nelson Betancourt makes his only Test appearance for West Indies, and captains the side, against England at Port of Spain. He is 42 years 242 days and scores 39 and 15 batting at No.9, but is not asked to repeat the feat!

1932 Don Bradman ends his innings v South Africa at Melbourne on 299*, then the highest Test score made in Australia and since bettered only by Bob Cowper's 307 at Melbourne in 1965–66. Going for 300, he runs out his last-man partner, H. Thurlow, for 0.

H.D.G. Leveson Gower, pioneer of festival cricket.

1954 Death of H.D.G. Leveson Gower at the age of 80. His name will always be linked with the English Cricket Festivals which traditionally closed the first-class season; many sides played as his XI.

1985 Mohammed Azharuddin sets a world record with his third century in his first three Tests, scoring 122 v England.

2

1892 Johnny Briggs (Lancashire) becomes the third bowler to perform the hat-trick in a Test, dismissing Australia's W.F. Giffen, Blackham and Callaway in the second Test at Sydney.

1973 Test début of Richard Hadlee, current record-holder for most Test wickets. Against Pakistan at Wellington the New Zealand paceman takes 2 for 84 and 0 for 28 and is dropped for the next Test, losing his place to his brother Dayle.

1988 David Boon's unbeaten 184 saves the day for Australia in the Bicentennial Test at Sydney.

3

1933 T.W. Wall (South Australia) takes 10 for 36 to bowl out New South Wales for 113 at Sydney – the first haul of 10 wickets in an innings in Sheffield Shield cricket.

1936 Birth of Bobby Simpson, captain of Australia 39 times, at Marrickville, Sydney. In 62 Tests he scores 4,869 runs at 46.81 with a best score of 311.

1974 Controversy at the Queen's Park Oval. After Julien plays the last ball of the day in the Test between West Indies and England, Tony Greig sees Kallicharran out of his ground and throws down the stumps at the bowler's end. Umpire David Sang Hue has no option but to give him out, though after heated discussion off the field the player, then on 142, is reinstated.

1984 Tony Pigott (Sussex) postpones his wedding day to play in the Test against New Zealand at Christchurch. This proves a wise decision for in 1989 he still awaits a further invitation to represent his country.

4

1895 Johnny Briggs (England) becomes the first player to take 100 Test wickets, against Australia at Sydney. Then C.T.B. Turner achieves the feat on the same day as England are bowled out twice for 65 and 72, losing by an innings and 147 runs.

1929 Archie Jackson (Australia) completes his maiden Test century v England at Adelaide. At 19 years 152 days he becomes the youngest person to score 100 in Tests between England and Australia.

1949 Everton Weekes (West Indies) completes a record run of seven Test fifties against India at Bombay. In the second innings he nearly makes it eight but is bowled by Hazare for 48.

1986 The Windward Islands beat England by seven wickets, their first victory over a touring side.

5

1889 Births of Patsy Hendren at Turnham Green and Ernest Tyldesley at Worsley, near Manchester. Hendren's career includes 170 centuries and 57,611 first-class runs, and Tyldesley scores more than 100 centuries and 38,874 first-class runs.

1930 On his 41st birthday Hendren scores 205* for England v West Indies at Port of Spain.

1970 John Traicos makes his début for South Africa in the second Test v Australia at Durban. After South Africa's expulsion from Test cricket, Traicos reappears in World Cup tournaments playing for next-door Zimbabwe.

Tim Robinson relaxes with other team members as England lose to the Windward Islands at St. Vincent.

FEBRUARY

FEBRUARY

6

1946   Clyde Walcott (314*) and Frank Worrell (255*) complete a world-record partnership of 574* playing for Barbados v Trinidad at Port of Spain.

1947   Arthur Morris scores 124* in Australia's second innings v England at Adelaide, completing a century double for the match; for England Denis Compton also scores two centuries – the only time two players have done this in the same Test match.

1953   Ian Craig makes his Test début for Australia at 17 years 239 days; he remains the youngest-ever Australian Test player.

1970   Graeme Pollock completes his innings of 274, the highest by a South African in Test cricket, v Australia at Durban.

7

1808   Birth of Tom Box, one of the first great wicket-keepers, in Sussex. A member of the Sussex team for nearly a quarter of a century, he is credited with 397 dismissals.

1857   Birth of dual cricket and soccer international Alfred Lyttelton, also a wicket-keeper. He plays cricket and soccer for Cambridge University and later joins Middlesex.

1952   A rest day is called in the Test between India and England at Madras to mourn the death of George VI.

8

1879   Pitch invasion at Sydney when W.L. Murdoch (New South Wales) is given run out by umpire George Coulthard against England. Coulthard is the official travelling umpire with the England team and Murdoch is on 82 when dismissed. Some England players are 'abused'.

1929   J.C. 'Farmer' White bowls a mean spell including 21 maidens to take 8 Australian wickets for 126 and secure victory for England by 12 runs in the Test at Adelaide.

1977   Waheed Mirza (324) and Mansoor Akhtar (224*) set a new world-record opening partnership. Playing for Karachi Whites against Quetta at Karachi, they put on 561 in 6½ hours, both making their maiden first-class centuries in the process.

J.C. White of Somerset and England.

Jim Laker, this time on the receiving end, as he is caught by Richie Benaud off Alan Davidson for 48 at Headingley in 1953.

9

1904 MCC bowl out Victoria for 15 in 42 minutes, the lowest first-class score in Australian cricket. Victorians wish to make it clear that their No.11, J.V. Saunders, did not bat.

1922 Birth of Jim Laker near Bradford, Yorkshire. Making his name in the great Surrey championship team of the 1950s, he is immortalized as the man who took 19 wickets in the Old Trafford Test in 1956.

1954 In five hours' play in the third day of the second Test against West Indies at Bridgetown, England amass 128 runs in 114 overs.

10

1847 Birth of Albert Hornby at Blackburn. He and A.E. Stoddart (see next entry) are the only men to captain England at cricket and Rugby Union.

1888 A.E. Stoddart makes his Test début for England v Australia. In the same year he is called upon to captain the touring British Lions Rugby team after the original captain R.L. Seddon is drowned in a boating accident in the Murray River.

1910 Birth of John Langridge, the long-serving Sussex batsman who holds the record for scoring the most centuries (76) without playing for England.

FEBRUARY

11

1882 W.L. Murdoch scores 321 for New South Wales v Victoria at Sydney, becoming the first Australian to pass 300 in a first-class innings and only the second man after W.G. Grace to do so.

1948 S.C. Griffith (England) scores his maiden first-class century on his Test début v West Indies at Port of Spain. Also appearing in his first Test is Frank Worrell, last of the 'Three Ws' to join the West Indies side.

1961 On the second day of the Australia v England Test at Melbourne the crowd of 90,800 is the largest ever to attend a Test match.

1961 Mushtaq Mohammad (Pakistan) becomes the youngest century-maker in Test cricket, scoring 101 v India at Madras at the age of 17 years 82 days.

Andy Ganteaume, a better Test average than the great Don Bradman.

12

1857 Birth of Robert Peel at Churwell, Leeds. The Yorkshire slow left-arm bowler plays 20 times for England but his drinking gets the better of him and Lord Hawke has to send him off the field for being drunk, so ending his career. Peel claimed 1,776 first-class wickets and 102 in Tests.

1949 Birth of Gundappa Viswanath at Bhadravati. The first to score a century (230) both on his first-class début and on his first appearance in a Test match (137), he played for India in 91 Tests.

1965 Graeme Pollock becomes the second player after George Headley to score three Test centuries before the age of 21, hitting 137 v England at Port Elizabeth.

13

1896 Test débuts for four England players v South Africa at Port Elizabeth: Lord Hawke, Tom Hayward and two noted all-rounders – C.B. Fry, who played soccer for England and held the world long-jump record, and S.M.J. Woods, who had played cricket for Australia and was also to play Rugby Union for England.

1948 Andy Ganteaume (West Indies) compiles a unique Test record, scoring 112 v England in his only innings in Test cricket.

1962 Barry Jarman, Australian wicket-keeper and one-time Test captain, dismisses 10 New South Wales batsmen - seven caught, three stumped – while playing for South Australia at Adelaide.

1970 Death of Herbert Strudwick at Shoreham, Sussex, aged 90. The Surrey and England wicket-keeper's career record includes 1,496 first-class dismissals and 72 in Test matches.

The young Pelham Warner, five years before his first Test appearance.

15

1921   Arthur Mailey takes 9 England wickets for 121 at Melbourne – the only instance of an Australian taking nine wickets in a Test innings.

1932   Australia dismiss South Africa for 45 in the second innings at Melbourne. Added to their first-innings score of 36, this gives them a match aggregate of 20 wickets for 81 runs.

1961   After losing the Test series to Australia, West Indies captain Frank Worrell presents the Worrell Trophy to his opposite number, Richie Benaud. The two countries still play for this trophy.

1980   England are dismissed for 64 by New Zealand at Wellington, their lowest score against New Zealand. The damage is done by Richard Hadlee who takes 6–26.

1980   Bob Taylor equals the world record for most dismissals in an innings in Test cricket when he claims seven Indian batsmen (all caught) in the Golden Jubilee Test at Bombay. His haul equals that made by Wasim Bari the previous year.

14

1888   Australia are dismissed for 42 by England at Sydney (Lohmann 5–17, Peel 5–18), their lowest Test score in their own country.

1896   Lohmann again. He takes 8 for 7 as South Africa are skittled for 30 at Port Elizabeth, and finishes the match with a hat-trick and final figures of 15–45. The South African total remains the lowest score in Test cricket for more than fifty years.

1899   P.F. (later Sir Pelham) Warner makes his Test début for England v South Africa at Johannesburg. Later in the match he becomes the first débutant to carry his bat through a completed innings for England, making 132*.

16

1933   England regain the Ashes in the 'Bodyline' series, beating Australia by six wickets at Brisbane with one match remaining.

1955   Miran Bux completes his Pakistan Test career after two matches. At the age of 47 years 302 he becomes the oldest Pakistani Test player, the oldest post-war Test player, and the sixth oldest of all-time.

1966   Bob Cowper completes his innings of 307 against England at Melbourne. Lasting 12 hours 7 minutes, it is the highest Test innings made in Australia.

MORNING FOODS LTD.

D. TALLON

A Series of 25
TEST CRICKETERS
England - Australia
Coronation Year - 1953

Issued by
Mornflake
QUICK COOKING **OATS**

No. 24
D. TALLON
(Queensland)
Don Tallon, born Bunda-
berg (Queensland) 17th
Feb., 1916. Entered first-
class cricket 1933. Has
played in 20 Tests. Height
5ft. 10½in., of medium build.
In his prime was described
as the finest wicket-keeper
in the world.
The best in any packet
MADE BY
MORNING FOODS LTD.
CREWE

17

1916 Birth of Don Tallon, one of Australia's finest wicket-keepers, at Bundaberg. He is unlucky in that his international career begins to peak at the outbreak of the Second World War.

1971 England beat Australia by 62 runs at Sydney and regain the Ashes after a 12-year interval.

1973 R.E. Redmond (New Zealand) scores 107 v Pakistan at Auckland on his Test début. In the second innings he completes his Test career with a top-scoring 56.

1982 First day of Sri Lanka's first Test match, v England at Colombo.

18

1914 S.F. Barnes (England) takes his series haul against South Africa to 49 wickets, a world record. With 7 for 56 and 7 for 88 in the match at Durban he completes his distinguished Test career.

1969 Doug Walters (Australia) becomes the first to score a double century (242) and a century (100*) in the same Test, v West Indies at Sydney.

1977 Test débuts of two of the West Indians' great squad of match-winning fast bowlers, Colin Croft and Joel Garner, v Pakistan at Bridgetown.

The scoreboard at Colombo during Sri Lanka's first Test match against England.

Doug Walters on his way to a double century at Sydney in 1969.

1986 Mike Gatting's nose is broken by a ball from Malcolm Marshall in a one-day international in the West Indies and he returns to England for treatment.

19

1891 Birth of J.C. 'Farmer' White at Holford, Somerset. The slow left-arm bowler captains his county and, in three Tests out of 15 played, leads the England team.

1972 Glenn Turner (New Zealand) makes the highest score (228*) for a batsman carrying his bat in Test cricket, v West Indies at Kingston.

1980 Ian Botham completes a remarkable performance in the Jubilee Test, scoring 114 and turning in match figures of 13 for 106. Bob Taylor, England's wicket-keeper, takes 10 catches in the same match – a Test record.

20

1923 C.A.G. Russell (England) makes his second century of the match v South Africa at Durban. In his previous Test appearance he scores 96. He never plays Test cricket again.

1957 Hugh Tayfield takes 9 for 113 v England at Johannesburg, the best figures by a South African bowler in Test matches.

1974 Pakistan Test batsman, Aftab Baloch, completes the sixth highest first-class innings on record, 428 for Sind v Baluchistan. Batting for 9 hours 44 minutes he becomes the youngest man to hit a quadruple century.

Hugh Tayfield, always a problem to English batsmen.

FEBRUARY

21

1808 Birth of Henry Mills Grace, father of W.G., at Long Ashton, Somerset.

1974 Dennis Amiss completes one of his greatest innings, scoring 262* v West Indies at Kingston and allowing England to reach 432–9 in their second innings and force a draw.

1982 Keith Fletcher celebrates his last match as England captain with his only Test win, v Sri Lanka at Colombo.

1986 Richard Hadlee takes his 300th Test wicket, dismissing Australian captain Allan Border at Wellington.

22

1923 England secure their first series win for nine years when they win the decisive 5th Test against South Africa at Durban by 109 runs.

1932 George Headley (344*) and C.C. Passailaigue (261*) put on a world-record stand of 487* for the sixth wicket. They are playing for Jamaica v Lord Tennyson's XI at Kingston.

1977 Extras makes a record contribution to Pakistan's innings v West Indies in Barbados, scoring 68 out of 291.

23

1842 Birth of James Lillywhite, England's first captain, at West Hampnett, Sussex.

1968 Graham Dowling (New Zealand) scores 239, his country's highest innings until beaten by Glenn Turner, v India at Christchurch.

1979 Wasim Bari (Pakistan) sets a record for Test wicket-keepers when he catches seven New Zealand batsmen in an innings at Auckland.

24

1931 Birth of Brian Close at Rawdon, near Leeds. The youngest man to play Test cricket for England (aged 18), his career extends across five decades and includes 34,911 first-class runs and 1168 wickets.

Brian Close during his highest first-class innings of 198 against Surrey.

1936 C.L. Badcock hits 325 for South Australia in the Sheffield Shield match v Victoria at Adelaide.

1949 Birth of John Lever at Stepney. The Essex medium-fast left-hander is still adding to his 1696 wickets in first-class cricket (at last reckoning).

1951 Birth of one of the game's great characters, Derek Randall, at Retford. The most famous innings of the Notts and England batsman (and acrobatic fielder) is his 174 in the Centenary Test at Melbourne.

FEBRUARY

John Arlott with the West Indian philosopher and cricket-writer C.L.R. James in 1964.

Derek Randall, following the flight of a six against the Australians at Lord's in 1977.

25

1914   Birth of the 'Voice of Cricket' and wine lover John Arlott at Basingstoke, Hampshire. Now retired to Alderney, he is one of the game's most knowledgeable authorities, his countryman's delivery the most imitated of all radio commentators.

1930   George Headley (West Indies) completes his second century of the match v England at Georgetown and becomes the first West Indian to achieve this feat and the first man to hit three Test centuries before his 21st birthday.

1938   Birth of Farokh Engineer at Bombay. Capped for India 46 times, the popular wicket-keeper is a favourite with Lancashire crowds and claims 824 first-class dismissals and 13,436 runs.

FEBRUARY

The three 'W's – Everton Weekes (right) with Frank Worrell (left) and Clyde Walcott.

Peter Willey bowls at Antigua in 1981 while Viv Richards watches from the non-striker's end.

26

1887   George Lohmann collects figures of 25–12–35–8 for England v Australia at Sydney, the first-ever eight-wicket haul in Test cricket.

1925   Birth of Everton Weekes at Bridgetown. A central figure of West Indies cricket in the 1950s, and one of the immortal 'Three Ws', he scores 4455 Test runs at 58.61.

1930   West Indies, captained by M.P. Fernandes, win their first Test match, beating England at Georgetown by 289 runs.

27

1914   Two pairs of brothers play for South Africa v England at Port Elizabeth: H.W. and D. Taylor, and P.A.M. and R.H.M. Hands.

1925   Clarrie Grimmett (Australia) makes an ominous Test début with 5 for 45 and 6 for 37 v England at Sydney, the first of his then record haul of 216 Test wickets.

1975   Death of Sir Neville Cardus at 85. His cricket and music writing for the *Manchester Guardian* set him at the very top level of the game's observers.

1981   St John's, Antigua stages its first Test. England provide the opposition and local hero Viv Richards obliges the crowd with a century.

28

1965   Terry Jarvis, opening bat, makes his Test début for New Zealand v India at Madras and takes 125 minutes to score nine runs.

1967   Dennis Lindsay (South Africa) completes a world-record 24 catches in the series v Australia.

1978   New Zealand opening bowler Ewen Chatfield runs out Derek Randall at the non-striker's end with Randall on 13. Two years earlier, England physio Bernard Thomas gave Chatfield the kiss of life after he was felled by a ball from Peter Lever.

1980   Death of Middlesex and England spinner and perceptive cricket writer Ian Peebles, aged 72.

29

1904   The first scheduled Leap Year day of Test cricket is lost to rain at the Sydney Cricket Ground.

1908   Birth of Alf Gover at Epsom, Surrey. The Surrey and England fast bowler twice takes 200 wickets in a season and his cricket school at East Hill, Wandsworth becomes a world-famous centre of instruction.

1912   The second scheduled Leap Year day of Test cricket, also at the Sydney Cricket Ground, is again lost to rain.

1964   At last Test cricket on a Leap Year day, but even now only four hours play is possible as New Zealand entertain South Africa at Dunedin.

FEBRUARY

MARCH

1

1839 Formation of present Sussex CCC. They must wait 134 years to win their first major trophy, beating Worcestershire in the final of the inaugural Gillette Cup (1963).

1921 Australia complete their 5–0 whitewash of England, Arthur Mailey taking 36 wickets in the series and Gregory a record 15 catches.

1958 Gary Sobers completes his world record Test score of 365*, after adding 446 with C.C. Hunte for the second wicket v Pakistan at Kingston. West Indies declare after the record is secure (beating Hutton's 364) on 790 for 3.

2

1898 Joe Darling hits the fastest Australian Test century against England at Sydney (91 minutes).

1936 Beginning the day on 129, Don Bradman hits 369 for South Australia v Tasmania at Adelaide, with four sixes and 46 fours, the whole innings taking him 253 minutes.

1974 Greg Chappell (Australia) completes his innings of 247* v New Zealand at Wellington, part of a record Test aggregate for one match of 380. His brother Ian also scores two centuries in the match, the second time two brothers have performed the feat in first-class cricket, the first being R.E. and W.L. Foster (Worcestershire) in 1899.

3

1888 Birth of F.T. Mann, captain of Middlesex and England, like his son F.G. Their county/country double is equalled in 1988 by the Cowdreys, Colin and Chris.

1896 George Lonmann (England) takes 9–28 v South Africa at Johannesburg, the second-best Test haul in one innings after Jim Laker's 10–53 in 1956.

1934 Bob Crisp (Western Province) takes four wickets in four balls v Natal at Durban. Two years earlier he achieved the same feat v Griqualand West at Johannesburg and he is the only man to take four wickets in four balls twice.

1939 The 'Timeless Test' begins between South Africa and England at Durban. It continues until the 14th when the tourists' boat sails for London.

1978 Desmond Haynes and Gordon Greenidge begin their first opening partnership for West Indies and put on 87 v Australia at Port of Spain. They are to open together in more than 100 Test innings, a record partnership.

4

1963 Colin Cowdrey and A.C. Smith set a new Test record with a ninth-wicket partnership of 163; this remains the English record.

1977 Colin Croft (West Indies) produces his country's best-ever bowling figures of 8 for 29 v Pakistan at Port of Spain.

1983 Sri Lanka play their first Test match in New Zealand and their sixth in all Test cricket with their international squad depleted by a 25-year ban on 14 players who toured South Africa, and injuries to three other key players. They lose the match in three days by an innings and 25 runs.

An unusual venue for West Indian openers Gordon Greenidge and Desmond Haynes as they take the field at Stamford Bridge football ground in a floodlit match against Essex in 1980.

5

1865 Formation of present Worcestershire CCC.

1907 Birth of Brian Sellers at Keighley. As Yorkshire captain from 1933 to 1947 he guides the county to six Championships.

1965 G.E. Vivian (New Zealand) makes his first-class début in a Test match, v India at Calcutta, aged 19. The other débutant in the side, Brian Taylor, scores 105 and takes 5 for 86 and becomes the first player to score a century and take five wickets on his first Test appearance.

1971 Mike Procter completes his sixth consecutive first-class century, batting for Rhodesia against Western Province at Salisbury, so equalling the record of C.B. Fry and Don Bradman.

6

1929 Birth of David Sheppard at Reigate, Surrey. The future captain of Sussex and Bishop of Liverpool plays 22 times for England, scoring 1172 Test runs at 37.80.

1969 Colin Milburn (England) scores 139 v Pakistan at Karachi in his last Test innings; in a car crash in Northamptonshire a few weeks later he injures an eye and loses his sight in it.

1971 Sunil Gavaskar (India), the world's most prolific Test batsman, makes his début for his country v West Indies at Port of Spain and scores 65 and 67*.

1983 Sidath Wettimuny and his brother Mithra (Sri Lanka) open the innings v New Zealand at Christchurch, equalling the brotherly feats of W.G. and E.M. Grace (1880) and Hanif and Sadiq Mohammad (1969).

7

1920 Birth of Willie Watson at Bolton-on-Dearne. The Yorkshire left-hander becomes a dual international at cricket and soccer and is selected for the final stages of the soccer World Cup in 1950. His first-class record includes 25,670 runs at 39.86.

1952 Birth of Viv Richards at St John's, Antigua. The West Indies captain plays for Antigua in a World Cup soccer qualifying match, joins Somerset in 1974 and makes his Test début the following winter v India. For several years he is regarded as the world's best batsman.

1987 Sunil Gavaskar becomes the first batsman to score 10,000 Test runs, v Pakistan in his 124th Test match.

8

1904 Hugh Trumble (Australia) takes a hat-trick in his final Test, claiming the wickets of Bosanquet, Warner and Lilley and finishing with 7 for 28, v England at Melbourne. This is his second Test hat-trick.

1951 Birth of Philippe Henri (Phil) Edmonds in Lusaka, Northern Rhodesia (now Zambia). The Middlesex and England left-arm bowler becomes a controversial figure, retiring early to a business career which includes an updated version of country house cricket, organized like Pro-Am golf tournaments.

1978 Clive Radley, in his second Test, takes 594 minutes to score the slowest 150 on record in England's first innings against New Zealand at Auckland.

9

1887 Birth of Phil Mead in London. The Hampshire left-hander ranks fourth in the all-time list of runs scored (55,061 at 47.67) and in the number of centuries hit (153). He is capped 17 times by England.

1969 Riot stops play in the Karachi Test between Pakistan and England, with

MARCH

Phil Edmonds on tour in 1986 with David Gower, commentator Henry Blofeld and journalists Scyld Berry and Peter West.

the visitors on 502 for 7 and Alan Knott 96*. Fearing for their safety the England team withdraw from the match and the tour.

1970   Lee Irvine scores South Africa's last Test century, v Australia at Port Elizabeth. It is his 26th birthday.

1971   Jack Noreiga (West Indies) takes 9–95 v India at Port of Spain. The off-spinner, playing in his second Test, becomes the first West Indian to capture nine wickets in a Test innings.

1928   Birth of dual cricket and soccer international Arthur Milton at Bristol. Between 1948 and 1974 he amasses 32,150 first-class runs, nearly all of them

for Gloucestershire, at 33.73. On his début for England (6 caps) he scores a century and opens the batting with Rugby Union international M.J.K. Smith.

1970   South Africa win their last Test, v Australia at Port Elizabeth, by 323 runs and players such as R.G. and P.M. Pollock, Richards and Barlow officially disappear from international cricket.

1974   Lawrence Rowe, opening for West Indies, completes his innings of 302 v England at Bridgetown.

1978   Geoff Howarth scores a second century v England at Auckland, the only New Zealander after Glenn Turner to achieve this feat.

1982   Salim Malik scores a century on his début for Pakistan v Sri Lanka at Karachi. At 18 years 328 days he is the youngest player to do so.

MARCH

11

1863 Birth of Andrew Stoddart at South Shields. A dual cricket and Rugby Union international, he leads England on two cricket tours to Australia. In 1886 he scores 485 for Hampstead against Stoics, then the highest score in any class of cricket.

1915 Birth of Vijay Hazare at Sangli, Maharashtra. With Gul Mahomed in 1947 he puts on a world record 4th wicket partnership of 577 runs for Baroda v Holkar at Baroda. In his 30 Tests he scores 2192 runs at 47.65.

1949 Last day of the record-breaking match between Bombay and Maharashtra at Poona, when 2376 runs are scored for 38 wickets.

1980 Taslim Arif scores 210* for Pakistan v Australia at Faisalabad. This is the last-but-one Test appearance of the opening bat and wicket-keeper, usually Wasim Bari's deputy. In his total of six Tests he scores 510 runs and finishes with an average of 62.52.

West Indian and Australian cricketers visit the grave of Sir Frank Worrell on the anniversary of his death, during their 1973 Test series.

12

1889 Hon. C.J. Coventry and B.A.F. Grieve (England) make their Test and first-class débuts v South Africa at Port Elizabeth. It is also the only Test appearance of the England captain, C. Aubrey Smith, who takes 5–19 and 2–42.

1977 First day of the Centenary Test at Melbourne. Australia are to repeat their victory in the first-ever Test match by the same margin – 45 runs.

1983 Clive Lloyd becomes only the third West Indian to score over 6,000 runs in Test cricket during the 2nd Test against India at Port-of-Spain.

13

1967 Death of Sir Frank Worrell from leukaemia at the age of 42. He plays in 51 Tests and scores 3860 runs at 49.48; in 1964 he is knighted for his services to cricket.

1974 Glenn Turner becomes the first New Zealander to score a century in each innings of a Test. His innings of 101 and 110* at Christchurch guide New Zealand to their first win against Australia.

1981 Roland Butcher becomes the first black player of West Indian extraction to play for England, v West Indies at Bridgetown.

Roland Butcher and Geoffrey Boycott leave Heathrow on their way to the West Indies in 1981.

NOTTINGHAMSHIRE BOWLERS

ALFRED SHAW

Alfred Shaw, bowler of the first ball in Test cricket.

14

1939   End of the 'Timeless Test' which began on the 3rd. The total of runs scored in the match, 1981, is the highest in Test cricket. England, chasing 696, reach 654–5 but then must leave to catch their boat.

1969   Seymour Nurse scores 258 for West Indies v New Zealand at Christchurch, the highest Test innings at the Lancaster Park ground. It is Nurse's final Test.

1986   Mike Gatting, having returned to the West Indies tour after having his nose broken by a ball from Malcolm Marshall, now collects a broken thumb off a delivery by Vibert Greene.

15

1877   First day of first-ever Test, Australia v England at Melbourne. Alfred Shaw bowls the first ball to Charles Bannerman who hits the first Test century (165). It is, of course, début day for all the players, one of whom, James Southerton, remains the oldest Test débutant at 49 years 119 days.

1963   Fred Trueman dismisses B.W. Sinclair (New Zealand) at Christchurch to pass Brian Statham's world record of 242 Test wickets. Trueman finishes with 307 wickets and Statham increases his total to 252.

1979   On the final day v Pakistan at Melbourne, Australia need 77 runs to win with seven wickets standing. In 33 balls Sarfraz Nawaz takes all seven wickets for one run, completing a Pakistan best of 9–86.

MARCH

16

1929 At the end of the first eight-day Test, Australia beat England at Melbourne by five wickets despite taking 271.3 overs to score 491 in their first innings.

1971 Death of 'Chuck' Fleetwood-Smith in Melbourne, aged 60. A fine left-arm spinner, his Test averages receive massive damage in the 'Hutton Test'; in the England innings of 903–7 he records 1–298, the 'worst' bowling figures in Test history.

1987 Graeme Pollock's last day in first-class cricket. Playing for Transvaal v Western Province in the Currie Cup final he is not out on 63 when rain ends play.

The bowling figures for Australia in the 1938 Test at The Oval.

17

1804 Birth of Fuller Pilch in Norfolk, one of the greatest of the early cricketers. He makes his name as a batsman with Kent, Hampshire, Surrey and Norfolk, scoring 10 centuries – very hard to do in those days and much more than any of his contemporaries.

1951 Brian Statham (England), for a period holder of the world record for Test wickets – after Alec Bedser's 236 and before Fred Trueman's 243 – makes his Test début v New Zealand at Christchurch.

1977 England fall short of the 463 required to win the Centenary Test at Melbourne, despite the magnificent 174 of Derek Randall, scored in 448 minutes and costing him many bruises in his battle to keep out Dennis Lillee.

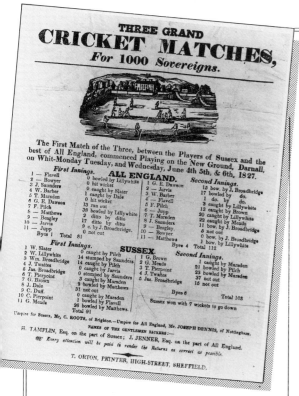

Fuller Pilch plays for All England against Sussex in 1827.

Gary Sobers and Colin Cowdrey before the Port of Spain Test in 1968.

18

1877   Birth of Clem Hill at Adelaide. One of seven brothers to play for South Australia, he enters the world while the first-ever Test match is in progress. As a left-handed bat he scores 17,213 first-class runs at 43.57 and plays 49 times for Australia.

1935   Patsy Hendren's last Test at the age of 46. In a versatile career he also plays soccer for Brentford and Manchester City and is capped in a 'Victory' international.

1954   Two of the Ws, Everton Weekes (206) and Frank Worrell (167), complete a stand of 338 for the 3rd wicket in the West Indies v England Test at Port of Spain.

19

1948   Birth of Vintcent van der Bijl at Cape Town. Arriving in England, the 6ft 8in medium-fast bowler is a great success at Middlesex and helps them to win the County Championship in 1980.

1958   Gary Sobers completes his second century in the Test v Pakistan at Georgetown. This brings his aggregate for the last three innings of the series to 599, for once out.

1968   Sobers makes a famous miscalculation at Port of Spain, declaring in the second innings at 92 for 2 and allowing England to gain a seven-wicket victory. This is the first victory in 19 years by a team batting fourth after a second-innings declaration and only the fourth instance ever.

MARCH

20

1850 Birth of Charles Thornton in Herefordshire. The man responsible for founding the Scarborough Festival, he plays first-class cricket for Cambridge University, Kent and Middlesex, entertaining the crowds with his big hits including nine sixes in one innings for Kent v Sussex at Tunbridge Wells.

The big-hitting Charles Thornton.

1886 Wellington are bowled out by Nelson for 19, after scoring 36 in their first innings. Nelson win by an innings and 46 runs, and their most successful bowler is A.P. Bennett with 6–13 and 6–5.

1965 S. Venkataraghavan (India) takes 8 for 72 v New Zealand at Delhi, and in the match bowls 122.3 overs including 56 maidens.

21

1892 Three brothers Hearne play in the same Test, South Africa v England at Cape Town, and one brother is in the 'other' team. G.G. and A. Hearne play for England and F. Hearne makes his début for South Africa having played twice for England.

1971 Sunil Gavaskar scores his first Test century – 116 for India v West Indies at Georgetown. His record for Test centuries still stands – 34.

1988 In the Sheffield Shield final at 'the WACA' (Perth), Chris Matthews takes his 50th wicket of the season, only the fifth man to complete 50 in a Sheffield Shield season. The others are Leslie Fleetwood-Smith, 60; Joel Garner, 55: Bill O'Reilly, 52; Tony Lock, 51.

22

1892 J.J. Ferris takes 7–37 in South Africa's second innings to complete a match analysis of 13–91. This is his only appearance for England, having previously played in eight Tests for Australia.

1947 In his last Test innings Walter Hammond (England) scores 79 v New Zealand at Christchurch.

1988 Ian Botham's last day as a Queensland player. He is to be sacked for an incident on the flight to Perth before the Sheffield Shield final which his team lose.

23

1896 George Lohmann (England) completes the remarkable series analysis of 35 wickets at 5.80 v South Africa.

1948 Birth of Wasim Bari at Karachi. In 1978–79 the Pakistan wicket-keeper makes seven dismissals in an innings, a world record shared with Bob Taylor (England). In all he dismisses 201 batsmen in Test cricket.

1980 Allan Border (Australia) becomes the first man to score 150 in both innings of a Test. He sets the record with 153 in the second innings v Pakistan at Lahore.

2 4

1892 A.E. Stoddart scores 134 in England's 499 at Adelaide, and England go on to record their largest winning margin against Australia – an innings and 230 runs – until the Oval Test of 1938.

1932 Death of Lord Harris at Belmont, aged 81. Described as the world's leading cricket missionary, he leads a team to Australia, encourages the game to grow in India when Governor of the country, is President of Kent and MCC, and plays with distinction for Kent and England.

1933 D.L. Freeman, right-arm googly bowler, makes his début for New Zealand at 18 years 197 days, the youngest débutant for that country.

2 5

1879 Formation of present Leicestershire CCC. They must wait 93 years to win their first major trophy, the Benson & Hedges Cup in 1972.

1885 England field an unchanged side through a five-match series with Australia!

1889 W.H. Ashley bowls for South Africa for the only time in a Test and takes 7 for 95 v England at Cape Town.

2 6

1889 Two records in the South Africa v England Test at Cape Town. Bernard Tancred (South Africa) becomes the first man to carry his bat through a completed innings in a Test, remaining unbeaten with 26* out of 47. South Africa are dismissed twice that day and Johnny Briggs records the best return for one day in Test history: 19.1–11–17–7 and 14.2–5–11–8.

1916 Birth of Bill Edrich at Lingwood, Norfolk. The high point of the Middlesex and England all-rounder's career is the 1947 season when with Denis Compton he shatters batting records, Edrich scoring 12 centuries and 3539 runs. He scores 36,965 runs in his first-class career, at 42.39, and averages 40.00 in his 39 Tests.

1958 Death of Hampshire's Phil Mead at Bournemouth, aged 71, after losing his sight in later years.

Another Edrich-Compton partnership.

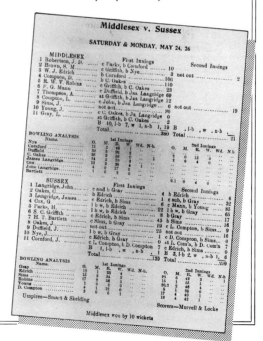

MARCH

27

1859 Birth of George Giffen at Adelaide. He is the only player not involved in county cricket to achieve the double of 10,000 runs and 1,000 wickets in first-class cricket (11,757 runs and 1022 wickets). In his most remarkable match, for South Australia v Victoria at Adelaide (where a stand is named after him), he scores 271 and takes 16 for 166 in the match.

1891 Birth of Vallence William Crisp Jupp at Burgess Hill, Sussex. He plays eight times for England, achieves the double twice for Sussex then joins Northamptonshire, for whom he achieves eight doubles, a record for an amateur player. He scores 23,296 first-class runs and takes 1658 wickets, and for years is the one class player in a struggling Northamptonshire side.

1973 Dennis Amiss is out for 99 in the Test between Pakistan and England at Karachi, the third player in the match to miss his century by one run, the others being Majid Khan (caught Amiss) and Mushtaq Mohammad (run out).

28

1926 Birth of Polly Umrigar at Bombay. The Indian all-rounder plays 59 times for his country, scoring 3631 Test runs at 42.22.

1951 Alex Moir bowls two consecutive overs v England at Wellington: the last before tea and the first after the interval.

1955 New Zealand register the lowest score in Test cricket – 26 all out v England at Auckland. Bert Sutcliffe is top scorer with 11, and Bob Appleyard is England's best bowler with 4–7.

1962 Lance Gibbs finishes the Indian innings at Bridgetown with a devastating spell of 15.3–14–6–8 and India slump from 158 for 2 to 187 all out.

29

1871 Birth of Tom Hayward at Cambridge. After playing for his home county he joins Surrey and in 1906 scores 3518 runs including 13 centuries. His record stands until the 1947 season of Compton and Edrich.

1946 Seven Australians make their débuts in the early post-war Test v New Zealand at Wellington, among them Ray Lindwall and Keith Miller. New Zealand are bowled out for 42 and 54, and Australia make 199 for 8 dec, the lowest run aggregate for a completed Test.

The prolific Tom Hayward.

1959   Wes Hall becomes the first West Indian bowler to perform the hat-trick in a Test, dismissing Mushtaq Mohammad, Fazal Mahmood and Nasim-ul-Ghani v Pakistan at Lahore.

30

1927   Birth of Wally Grout in North Queensland. He represents his country in 51 Tests and secures 187 dismissals. He is to die young, in 1968, from heart trouble.

1940   Birth of Norman Gifford in the Lake District. After 22 years with Worcestershire the left-arm spinner moves to Warwickshire in 1983 and takes 104 wickets in the season. He plays 15 times for England and takes 2068 first-class wickets at 23.56.

1954   Gary Sobers makes his Test début at 17 years 245 days, the second youngest

to play for his country. Played as a slow left-arm bowler he takes 4–81 in the match, contributing 14* and 29 with the bat.

31

1946   Birth in India of Aftab Gul, future Test player with Pakistan. His critics claim that, as a student leader, he is included in Test teams to pacify unruly crowds, though his 6149 first-class runs at 36.92 suggest he is worth his place.

1978   After the suspension of the Packer players, six new caps appear for West Indies v Australia at Georgetown. Among them are Sylvester Clarke and Basil 'Shotgun' Williams who scores 10 and 100.

1988   Dennis Lillee formally becomes a Northamptonshire player.

APRIL

1

1933   Walter Hammond passes Bradman's record score in Test cricket (334), completing 336* v New Zealand at Auckland, of which 295 are scored on this day. The innings is the fastest triple century in Test cricket.

1935   Birth of John Murray in Kensington, London. The Middlesex and England wicket-keeper becomes, in 1957, the second player after Les Ames to perform the 'keeper's double of 1000 runs and 100 dismissals. He is awarded the MBE for his services to cricket.

1957   Birth of David Gower at Tunbridge Wells. The Leicestershire and England captain appears in 51 consecutive Tests between 1981 and 1986 and in 1988 reaches 7000 Test runs in his 100th Test.

2

1933   Death of K.S. Ranjitsinhji, His Highness the Jam Sahib of Nawanagar, aged 60. In 1899 he becomes the first to score more than 3000 runs in a season (3159) and in first-class cricket for Cambridge University and Sussex he scores 24,692 runs at 56.37; for England he plays in 15 Tests, scoring 989 runs at 44.95.

1946   Birth of Dick Collinge at Wellington. The New Zealand medium-fast bowler holds two Test records – for batting. In 1972–73 he and Brian Hastings put on 151 for the 10th wicket v Pakistan at Auckland, and his 68* is a record for a No.11.

1954   Len Hutton (England) completes a marathon 205 in 538 minutes v West Indies at Kingston, and thanks largely to him England win the match by nine wickets and square the series 2–2 after being 0–2 down.

3

1849   Formation of the first Hampshire CCC. The present club is formed 14 years later.

1899   South African Jimmy Sinclair becomes the first man to score a century (106) and take six wickets (6–26) in the first innings of a Test, v England at Cape Town. His innings is also South Africa's first Test century.

1988   Confusion over the birthday of Sir Neville Cardus. His centenary is celebrated on this day though the records say his date of birth is 2nd April 1889.

David Gower reaches 50 against India in 1979.

APRIL

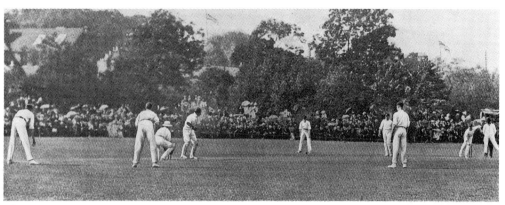

Alec Hearne of Kent bowls to K.S. Ranjitsinhji at Tonbridge. C.B. Fry is the Sussex batsman at the non-striker's end.

4

1899 South Africa are bowled out by England for 35 in 114 balls, the fourth lowest total in Test cricket.

1953 Birth of Henry Fotheringham, stalwart opening bat for Transvaal and unofficial South African teams.

1957 Birth of Paul Downton at Farnborough, Kent. While still deputy at Kent to Alan Knott he is selected to tour

Sir Neville Cardus.

with England, then moves to Middlesex and establishes himself as England wicket-keeper.

5

1884 Death of John Wisden at Westminster, aged 57. The founder of the famous Cricketers' Almanack was no mean cricketer, taking all 10 wickets for North v South at Lord's in 1850.

1890 First day of first Currie Cup final, at Kimberley, between Kimberley and Transvaal. Transvaal win and take the Cup.

1911 First MCC touring team to West Indies complete the only tied match in the Caribbean (Jamaica 173 and 227, MCC 269 and 131).

1930 England are bowled out for 849 on the third day v West Indies at Kingston. Sandham (325) makes a new highest individual Test score and Les Ames (149) scores the first Test century by a wicket-keeper.

1938 Birth of Colin Bland at Bulawayo, Rhodesia. The right-handed bat and brilliant cover point plays 21 times for South Africa, scoring 7249 first-class runs at 37.95.

APRIL

1956 Birth of Dilip Vengsarkar at Rajapur. The Indian right-hander becomes, in 1979, one of three Indians to score more than 1000 Test runs in a calendar year, the others being Gavaskar and Viswanath. Also born on this day is Mudassar Nazar, Pakistan's long-serving all-rounder.

1971 Sunil Gavaskar scores 117* in the final day of the 4th Test against the West Indies at Georgetown. This helps India to hold out for a draw and so secure their first-ever series win in the Caribbean.

1972 Alvin Kallicharran makes his Test début for West Indies against New Zealand at Georgetown. He goes on to score 100* in his first Test innings.

1973 Clive Lloyd scores 178 against Australia at Georgetown, his highest Test innings in the Caribbean.

Alvin Kallicharran in conversation with Alan Oakman before his first season at Warwickshire in 1971.

1889 Death of Henry Jupp, England's top-scorer in the first Test match at Melbourne in 1877.

1902 Birth of Arthur Wellard at Southfleet, Kent. A fast bowler renowned also for his hitting, the Somerset and England player sets a record in 1935 for hitting 66 sixes in a season, bettered only fifty years later by Ian Botham (80).

1957 Death of Frank Chester, best umpire of his day, aged 62. He took up umpiring in his twenties after losing an arm in the First World War.

1882 Birth of Bert 'Dainty' Ironmonger in Queensland. The left-arm medium-pacer, nicknamed for his clumsy fielding, makes his Test début at the age of 46 years 237 days and begins his final Test at 50 years 327 days, making him the oldest player to appear for Australia. In his 14 Tests he takes 74 wickets at 17.97.

1943 Birth of Dennis Amiss in Birmingham. The Warwickshire batsman's 43,423 first-class runs, on his retirement at the end of 1987, is the eleventh best of all time and his 7040 runs in the Sunday League is a record. In his 50 Tests he scores 3612 runs at 46.30.

1962 Polly Umrigar hits a magnificent 172* out of 230 in 248 minutes v West Indies at Port of Spain, before he runs out of partners.

1946 Birth of Alan Knott at Belvedere. The Kent and England wicket-keeper makes his county début at 18 and is soon renowned for his enthusiastic 'keeping, constant physical jerks on the field and conscientious batting in the lower middle order, where he many times rescues his country.

APRIL

1972 New Zealanders Glenn Turner and Terry Jarvis complete a stand of 387 for the 1st wicket v West Indies at Georgetown. Turner's 259 is the highest individual score for New Zealand and the partnership is the second-highest for the 1st wicket in Test cricket.

1984 Local heroes Viv Richards (178) and Richie Richardson (154) share in a stand which eventually totals 308 for West Indies v Australia at St John's, Antigua.

10

1927 Death of Hon. Ivo Bligh at Cobham, Kent, aged 68. Bligh is famous for being the first man to lead an England side to Australia and attempt to 'regain' the Ashes (1882–83). As Lord Darnley he becomes President of the MCC and after his death his widow presents the urn containing his ashes to the MCC.

1930 George Headley scores 223 for West Indies v England at Kingston. He is the youngest to score a double century in a Test until Javed Miandad, and the first to score four Test centuries before the age of 21.

1988 Death of Cliff Gladwin, Derby and England bowler. Playing for his county between 1939 and 1958 he takes 1536 first-class wickets at 17.67.

Hon. Ivo Bligh with the team which he led to Australia in 1882–83.

APRIL

1856   Birth of Arthur Shrewsbury. The great Notts professional becomes a mainstay of the England team, helping to manage three tours to Australia. In 1887–88 he is the first outfielder to hold six catches in a Test match. His first-class run aggregate, 26,505, is remarkable for its time (1875–1902), as is his average, 36.65.

1921   Birth of Jeffrey Stollmeyer near Port of Spain, Trinidad. This fine opening batsman on the West Indies' victorious tour of England in 1950 later becomes a senior administrator in the game. In 1946–47 he hits the highest score for Trinidad, 324 v British Guiana at Port of Spain.

1955   Turf is introduced at Port of Spain, ostensibly to give the bowlers a chance. The first Test played on the new surface, West Indies v Australia, yields 1255 runs for 23 wickets! Gary Sobers begins a world-record run of 85 consecutive Test match appearances.

SHAW AND SHREWSBURY'S TEAM OF 1884-5.

1. *M. Read.*   5. *Joe Hunter.*   10. *J. Lillywhite.*
2. *G. Ulyett.*   6. *W. Attewell.*   11. *W. Flowers.*
3. *W. Scotton.*   7. *A. Shrewsbury.*   12. *J. Briggs.*
4. *R. Peel.*   8. *Alfred Shaw (Capt.).*   13. *W. Bates.*
   9. *W. Barnes.*

The Shaw and Shrewsbury team to Australia in 1884–85.

1917   Birth of Vinoo Mankad in Jamnagar. The finest Indian all-rounder before Kapil Dev, he scores 2109 runs and takes 162 Test wickets in 44 appearances.

1930   The ninth scheduled day of play in the West Indies v England Test at Kingston is abandoned and the match declared a draw. The day marks the end of a great Test career lasting a record 31 years 315 days, that of Wilfred Rhodes who at 52 years 165 days is the oldest man selected to play Test cricket. Also making his final appearance, in the pavilion if not on the field of play, is the third oldest Test player, George Gunn, aged 50 years 303 days.

1976   India beat West Indies by 6 wickets at Port of Spain, scoring a record match-winning fourth-innings total of 406–4 (Gavaskar 102, M.B. Amarnath 85, Viswanath 112).

1962   Gary Sobers scores 104 on the first day of the 5th Test at Kingston to lay the foundations for a fifth successive victory over India to record the third 5–0 whitewash in Test history.

1971   A misunderstanding leads to both captains, Gary Sobers (West Indies) and Ajit Wadekar (India), thinking they have won the toss at Port of Spain. Each wants to bat on the fine strip, but Sobers eventually concedes first use to the visitors.

14

1867 Birth of Sammy Woods at Ashfield, New South Wales. The great all-rounder joins Somerset, plays three times for Australia then plays three Tests for England. In between he turns out 13 times for England at Rugby Union. His career averages reveal an impressive combination: 15,345 runs at 23.42 and 1040 wickets at 20.82.

1947 Birth of Bob Massie at Perth. His Test début v England at Lord's in 1972 is one of the most spectacular of all time: spells of unplayable swing bowling from round the wicket bring him 8–84 and 8–53.

1965 Gerry Gomez, a current West Indian Test selector, is appointed to stand as umpire in the 3rd Test against Australia at Georgetown after C.P. Kippins withdraws on the eve of the Test.

15

1845 Birth of David Gregory near Sydney. Australia's first Test captain is an imposing 14-stoner, a hard-hitting batsman and keen slip-fielder. His brother Ned also plays in the inaugural Test.

1938 Alec and Eric Bedser pass through the gates of The Oval to begin their careers with Surrey CCC.

1986 Viv Richards hits the fastest-ever Test century measured in balls received (56), v England at Antigua, his home island. Although not amazingly rapid in time taken (81 minutes), the number of balls faced is 11 less than the previous record, set by J.M. Gregory in 1921–22.

Sammy Woods captains the Somerset side of 1896.

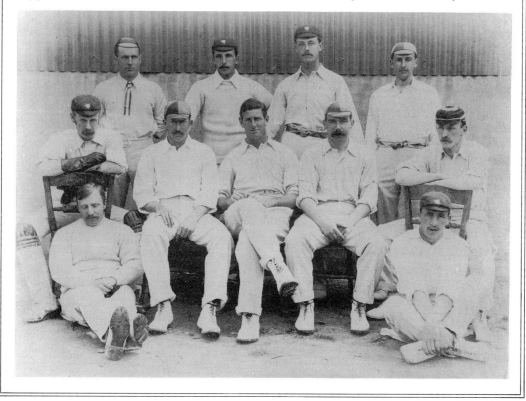

APRIL

16

1878 Birth of R.E. Foster at Malvern. Third of the seven brothers who play for Worcestershire, in 1903–4 he sets an individual Test record of 287 on his début v Australia which lasts for 26 years. With Wilfred Rhodes he puts on 130 for the last wicket, and that record lasts for 69 years.

1940 Birth of David Holford at Bridgetown. Although popularly known for being Gary Sobers's cousin he proves good enough in his own right to play 22 times for West Indies. At Lord's in 1966 he adds 274 with Sobers, scoring 105* and helping to save the match.

1986 West Indies beat England at St John's, Antigua to win the series 5–0 and thereby complete the alarming phenomenon known as Blackwash 2.

17

1944 Death of J.T. Hearne at Chalfont St Giles, Buckinghamshire, aged 76. Fourth on the all-time list of wicket-takers his total haul is 3061; in 1896 he reached 100 wickets on 12th June, the earliest date for the bowler's century.

1961 Birth of Norman Cowans in Enfield, Jamaica. Nineteen years later he makes his first-class début for Middlesex and in 1982 is selected to tour Australia, playing in his first Test match at Perth.

1978 Derek Parry scores 65, batting at No 8, to set up a West Indies win against Australia at Port-of-Spain. He follows this with 5–15 to bowl out Australia for 94.

18

1958 Birth of Malcolm Marshall at Barbados. The West Indian paceman rises to become the world's most feared and successful fast bowler. Joining Hampshire in 1979, he takes a record 134 wickets in 1982, the best since the reduction in number of Championship matches.

1980 A famous Benson & Hedges match at Taunton, where Middlesex score 282 for 6 (Gatting 95*, Barlow 93) and Somerset 281 for 8 (Gavaskar 123).

1988 Peter Bowler (155* v Cambridge University at Fenner's) becomes the first to score a début century for two counties. The Derbyshire opener hit 100* on his first appearance for Leicestershire in 1986, v Hampshire at Leicester.

Peter Bowler – a unique achievement.

19

1873 Birth at Smethwick of Sydney Barnes , possibly the best bowler of all time. He plays in 27 Tests for England, and v South Africa in 1913–14 takes a record 49 wickets in the series.

1933   Birth of Bird: Umpire Dickie. The only man to officiate in 100 internationals, he plays for Yorkshire and Leicestershire before settling down to become the world's best-known umpire.

1971   Sunil Gavaskar finishes the series v West Indies with 774 runs at 154.80, a world record for a player in his first series. His batting ensures that India win their first rubber in the West Indies. In the second innings Gavaskar completes a double century (220) and this, added to his 124 in the first innings, makes him the second man in Test history (after Doug Walters) to score a century and double century in the same Test.

1987   Brendon Kuruppu (Sri Lanka) scores 201 on his Test début v New Zealand at Colombo. It takes him 777 minutes, the longest double century in Test cricket and the third longest innings of all time.

APRIL

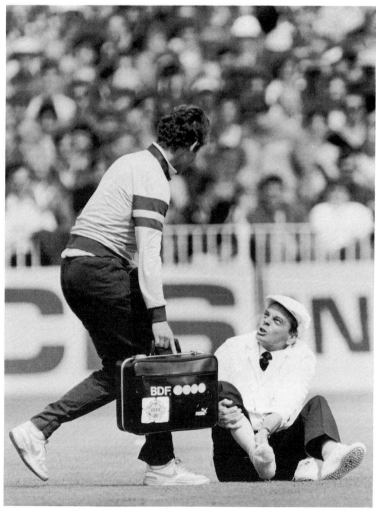

Dickie Bird receives attention at Old Trafford in 1985 after being hit by a shot from Graham Gooch.

APRIL

20

1954 Birth of Peter Toohey in New South Wales. The right-handed bat comes to prominence when Packer's Australian stars are not available for selection. He plays 15 times for his country without ever quite establishing himself. Happily for him, cricket is a form of relaxation; his family own Toohey's Breweries, one of the largest in the country.

1972 Alvin Kallicharran adds a second successive Test century (101) to his début 100*, v New Zealand at Port of Spain.

1972 Gary Sobers becomes the first captain 'to win' all five tosses in a series for the second time. He also sets a world record (later to be passed by G.R. Viswanath of India) by making his 85th consecutive Test appearance.

21

1838 Birth of Nathaniel Thompson in Birmingham, England. As an Australian opening bat he goes down in history for being the first man dismissed in Test cricket, bowled by Allen Hill for 1 in the inaugural Test at Melbourne in 1877.

1919 Birth of John Goddard at Bridgetown. As West Indies captain his finest hour arrives in 1950 when he leads his country to a 3–1 series win over Norman Yardley's England side.

1987 New Zealand call off the Test v Sri Lanka because they fear for the players' safety as the political situation worsens and a nearby bomb kills 150.

1988 First day of the new four-day matches in the County Championship.

22

1937 Birth of 'Umpire Ken Palmer'. The Somerset all-rounder plays county cricket for 15 seasons (7567 runs and 837 wickets) and plays one Test for England, called into the side v South Africa while coaching in Johannesburg, in 1964–65. Now a familiar figure to television viewers as well as live crowds at Test match grounds.

1983 A new Test venue enters the calendar – Kandy, where Sri Lanka are hosts to Australia.

1987 Wayne Daniel (Middlesex) returns the best-ever Benson & Hedges Cup bowling figures with 7 for 12 v Minor Counties (East) at Ipswich.

23

1929 F.C. Toone, Secretary of Yorkshire CCC, is knighted for his services to cricket. These include taking three tours to Australia.

1937 Birth of Barrie Shepherd in Western Australia. He captains his State side for several seasons, and as an opening bat for Australia scores 502 Test runs at 41.83.

1986 Death of Jim Laker, aged 64. In later life the holder of the finest bowling figures in cricket – 19 for 90 v Australia in 1956 – became a much respected commentator with BBC Television.

1988 Graham Gooch (Essex) hits a career-best 275 v Kent at Chelmsford, including four sixes and 27 fours. It is the highest score ever made in April in England.

2 4

1905 Jack Hobbs makes his first-class début for Surrey v Gentlemen of England at The Oval. He scores 18 and 88.

A young Jack Hobbs before the First World War.

1940 Birth of David Larter at Inverness, Scotland. The 6ft 8in fast bowler joins Northants and many look to him as the successor to Frank Tyson. He plays in 10 Tests but continual injuries harass his career and force him to retire from the game.

1979 The Australian Broadcasting Corporation grant Kerry Packer exclusive rights to screen matches arranged by the Australian Cricket Board for 10 years. This ensures the demise of his World Series Cricket which has divided the sport into bitterly opposed factions.

1987 The anxious New Zealand team abandon their tour of Sri Lanka, having called off the Colombo Test on the 21st.

2 5

1872 Birth of C.B. Fry in Croydon, Surrey. One of sport's greatest all-rounders, his feats include playing first-class and Test cricket; playing soccer for England and appearing in an FA Cup final; equalling the world long-jump record; playing Rugby Union with the Barbarians. In the political arena he stands three times as a Liberal candidate and is once offered the throne of Albania. In his first-class cricket, mainly for Sussex, he scores 30,886 runs at 50.22.

1930 Birth of Roy Marshall in Barbados. The bespectacled Hampshire and West Indies opener is renowned for his attacking style which brings him 35,725 first-class runs at 35.94, including 68 centuries.

1976 India, with five wickets down for 97 in their second innings v West Indies at Kingston, are forced to close the innings because five players are absent hurt. West Indies score the 13 runs required to win without loss. Afterwards, the Indians remain upset by the short-pitched bowling tactics of their hosts, which accounted for injuries in the first innings to Gaekwad, Viswanath and Patel. The other two absent players are Bedi and Chandrasekhar.

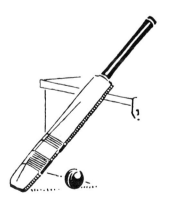

APRIL

26

1909 Birth of Richard Howorth, of Worcestershire and England: he is to become a successful all-rounder, completing the double in 1939 and again in 1946 and 1947, but like many others loses six years of a promising career to the Second World War.

1973 Lance Gibbs, West Indies, and Max Walker, Australia, both take wickets on the final day of the 5th Test at Port of Spain to share a new record of 28 wickets for an Australian series in the West Indies.

1983 Sri Lanka lose their first Test against Australia at Kandy and Greg Chappell has his last day as Australian captain after being in charge for 48 Tests.

27

1875 Birth of Freddie Fane in Ireland. Jack Hobbs's opening partner in his first Test, Fane stands in as England captain for three Tests on the 1907–8 tour of Australia when A.O. Jones is ill.

1973 Death of Jim Sims at Canterbury, aged 69. One of the great Middlesex stalwarts, he took 1581 wickets and hit four centuries.

1987 Death of V.M. Merchant in Bombay, one of India's first outstanding Test batsmen.

1988 Abdul Qadir (Pakistan) attacks a spectator who successfully goads the highly-strung leg-spinner during the final Test v West Indies at Bridgetown. Qadir admits the assault and is reprimanded.

28

1906 Birth of Les Berry at Dorking, Surrey. He scores a record 30,143 runs for Leicestershire in a 27-year career, including 2446 in 1937.

1908 Birth of Jack Fingleton at Sydney. One of the few who faced the Bodyline attack of the 1932–33 MCC tourists without complaint, the New South Wales opener is a prominent Test cricketer in

The demonstrative Abdul Qadir claims another victim.

the 1930s and then makes an even bigger name as a journalist and cricket writer.

1942   Birth of Mike Brearley, one of England's most successful captains, at Harrow. He leads his county, Middlesex, to four Championship successes and is England captain in 31 Tests.

1983   India's Laxman Sivaramakrishnan takes the field v West Indies at St John's, Antigua at 17 years 118 days, the fifth youngest Test cricketer of all time (the four ahead of him are all Pakistanis).

29

1895   Birth of Maurice Tate at Brighton. Like his father Fred he plays for Sussex and England, appearing in 39 Tests between 1925 and 1935, scoring 1198 runs and taking 155 wickets.

1918   Birth of Mervyn Harvey, little known elder brother of Neil who plays for Australia v England in the fourth Test in 1946–47 and puts on 116 with Arthur Morris for the 1st wicket in the second innings.

1930   Birth of Alf Valentine in Kingston, Jamaica. Immortalized in the calypso about the 1950 West Indies tour of England, he takes 123 wickets that summer including 33 in the Test series.

30

1905   Birth of W.W. Keeton at Shirebrook. The Notts opener plays in the last Test before the Second World War and continues to play county cricket until 1951, when he is 46 years old.

1983   Gordon Greenidge and Desmond Haynes add 286 for the West Indies 1st wicket v India at St John's, Antigua.

1988   Graeme Hick (Worcestershire) reaches a total of 410 first-class runs in first-class cricket – a record for April.

MAY

1

1929 Birth of Sonny Ramadhin at Trinidad. In 1950 the deadly partner of Alf Valentine (see 29th April), he takes a career total of 158 Test wickets at 28.98. In 1957, v England at Edgbaston, he delivers 774 balls in 129 overs, a record for a Test innings.

1949 Formation of Board of Control for Cricket in Pakistan, following the Partition of British India in 1947.

1951 Birth of Gordon Greenidge at Barbados. The Hampshire and West Indies opener makes his county début at the age of 19 and becomes an outstanding batsman at every level.

1980 Zimbabwe quit the South African Cricket Union.

2

1894 MCC defeat Sussex at Lord's in a single day. MCC make 105 (Stoddart 44) then dismiss Sussex for 42 and 59.

1901 Birth of R.E.S. Wyatt at Milford, Surrey. He plays for Warwickshire, Worcestershire and England, scoring 39,405 runs at 40.04. In 1932–33 he takes on the daunting task of vice-captain to Douglas Jardine on the Bodyline tour.

1963 Completion of the first Gillette Cup match – Lancs v Worcs at Old Trafford. Peter Marner (Lancs) scores the first Gillette century but the visitors win the match.

3

1945 Birth of Sadiq Mohammad, fifth cricketing member of a famous family, at Junagadh. He makes his first-class début at the age of 14 and goes on to play for

G.H.G. Doggart in the nets in 1948.

Gloucestershire and Pakistan. In 1976 he scores a century in four consecutive innings.

1948 Hubert Doggart scores 215* for Cambridge University v Lancashire at Fenner's. This is the highest score by a débutant in modern times.

1978 Australia are denied victory v West Indies at Kingston when the crowd invades the pitch 12 minutes from the close of play. Efforts to play the remaining 38 balls next day fail when umpire Gosein refuses to stand. The match is declared a draw.

4

1875 Birth of R.O. Schwartz at Lee, Kent. He plays for Middlesex then emigrates to South Africa. He returns in 1907 with the South African tourists to become a unique (at the time) dual international – having already played Rugby Union for England.

1969 Essex are quickly into their stride in the new Sunday League scoring 265 off their 40 overs against Lancashire on the second Sunday of the season. Keith Boyce scores 50 in 23 minutes.

1975 Bob Taylor (Derbyshire) dismisses seven Lancashire batsmen in a John Player League match – a world record for a one-day game.

5

1911 Birth of Norman Oldfield, successful batsman for both Lancashire (1935–39) and Northants (1948–54). He makes a promising Test début scoring 80 in his first innings against the West Indies at The Oval in 1939 but this is the last match before war breaks out and is to be Oldfield's only Test appearance.

1933 Birth of 'Collie' Smith at Kingston, Jamaica. The West Indian all-rounder scores more than 4000 first-class runs and takes 121 wickets, then at the age of 26 is killed in a car crash.

6

1676 The earliest reference to cricket outside Britain appears in the diary of naval chaplain Henry Teonge, after a visit to Aleppo, Syria. He refers to several games and pastimes enjoyed there – duck-hunting, fishing, shooting, hand-ball and 'krickett'.

1965 Bobby Simpson (201) and Bill Lawry (210) complete their record opening stand for Australia, 382 v West Indies at Bridgetown, and become the first opening pair in Test cricket each to score a double century.

1988 Zimbabwe-born Graeme Hick scores 405* for Worcestershire v Somerset at Taunton, the second highest first-class innings in England behind Archie MacLaren's 424, made in 1895, also at Taunton.

Graeme Hick during his innings of 405* at Taunton.

COMPLETE SERIES - 50.

Caricatures of Famous Cricketers

INCLUDING TEST TEAMS

No. 39. DULEEPSINHJI, K. S.
(Cambridge University.)

Born 1905, a nephew of K. S. Ranjitsinhji, member of Cambridge University, 1925. A batsman of undoubted ability, his placing to the on, being the best feature of his batting, scored 932 runs in 1925, average 49·05. Played for Gentlemen against Players at Lords and Scarborough, 1925. All being well, should be a Test Match player of the future. A good field.

ISSUED WITH

SUNDI

K.S.DULEEPSINJI.

Bobby Peel, top-scorer in Yorkshire's massive total, but more usually known as a bowler.

7

1900   Yorkshire beat Worcestershire by an innings and five runs at Bradford. Only 193 runs are scored.

1930   K.S. Duleepsinhji (Sussex) sets a county record with 333 v Northamptonshire at Hove. The runs are made out of 520 in 330 minutes with one six and 34 fours.

1949   John Dewes (214*) and Hubert Doggart (219*), playing for Cambridge University v Essex at Cambridge put on 429 for the 2nd wicket, an English first-class record that stands for 25 years.

8

1896   Yorkshire complete their innings of 887 v Warwickshire at Birmingham, the highest-ever in the County Championship. This is the first time four players score a century in the same innings: R. Peel 210*, Lord Hawke 166, E. Wainwright 126, F.S. Jackson 117.

1908   Northants are dismissed by Yorkshire at Northampton for 27 and 15 in 135 minutes, the lowest first-class aggregate in Britain (at the time).

1923   Jack Hobbs reaches his 100th hundred, scoring 116* v Somerset at Bath. He finishes his career with 197 centuries.

1942   Birth of Robin Hobbs at Chippenham, Wiltshire. Playing for Essex v Australians at Chelmsford in 1975, the leg-spinner hits a century in 44 minutes, the fifth fastest of all time (now the ninth fastest).

AUSTRALIAN
AND ENGLISH
TEST CRICKETERS
*A Series of Forty
Actual Photographs*

No. 40

G. DUCKWORTH.
(Lancashire.)
Born May 9th. 1901.

One of the best wicket keepers in England, being especially strong on the leg side. First played for Lancashire in 1923. In the last match between the Gentlemen v. Players at Lord's he caught six batsmen and stumped another. A fair batsman.

Issued by
MAJOR DRAPKIN & CO.
Branch of The United Kingdom
Tobacco Co. Ltd. LONDON.

1975   Keith Boyce scores a 70-minute century against Minor Counties South two days after his 58-minute century against Leicestershire in the County Championship.

11

1937   Pelham Warner is knighted for his services to cricket.

1944   Birth of John Benaud at Auburn, Sydney. Brother of Richie, he plays three times for Australia and scores 223 runs at 44.60.

9

1901   Birth of George Duckworth at Warrington, Lancashire. He keeps wicket for England on 24 occasions and is one of the great figures in county cricket between the Wars, making 424 first-class appearances for Lancashire.

1932   Birth of Conrad Hunte in Barbados. The West Indian opener scores 3245 Test runs at 45.06 and in 1957–58 puts on 446 for the 2nd wicket with Gary Sobers (365*) v Pakistan at Kingston, himself scoring a great if overshadowed 260.

1977   First announcement in England of Kerry Packer's cricket 'circus'. Thirty-five players are signed, 18 from Australia and 17 from overseas, selected by Ian Chappell and Tony Greig.

10

1930   Clarrie Grimmett takes all 10 Yorkshire wickets for 37 runs at Sheffield, the Australians bowling out the home side for 155.

1954   Death of George Hirst (Yorkshire and England) at Huddersfield, aged 82. He is the only man to achieve the double of 2000 runs and 200 wickets in a season.

John Benaud, who surprisingly played only three times for Australia.

1955   Death of Gilbert Jessop at Fordington, Dorset. Nicknamed 'The Croucher' he was one of the biggest hitters in the game, scoring 26,698 runs for Cambridge University, Gloucestershire and England, with a best of 286 v Sussex at Hove in 1903.

MAY

12

1867 Birth of Hugh Trumble at Melbourne. One of the legendary early bowlers, he takes 141 Test wickets and, in his last appearance for Australia, v England at Melbourne in 1903, returns figures of 7 for 28 including a hat-trick.

1890 Jesse Hide (Sussex) takes 7–22 including four wickets in four balls v MCC at Lord's.

1903 Birth of Jim (J.H.) Parks at Haywards Heath. He holds the unique record of scoring 300 runs and taking 100 wickets in a season (1937). Other cricketing members of the Parks family are his brother Harry (Sussex), son Jim (J.M.) (Sussex, Somerset and England) and grandson Bobby (Hampshire).

13

1872 G. Strachan (Surrey), aged 21 years 174 days, becomes the youngest regular county captain.

1890 Sammy Woods takes 10–69 for Cambridge University v C.I. Thornton's XI at Cambridge, the first time this feat has been performed there.

1946 Indian No.11 Shute Banerjee is dismissed for 121, ending a remarkable partnership with No.10 Chandu Sarwate (124*) v Surrey at The Oval. Their stand of 249 is the first in first-class cricket in which Nos.10 and 11 each score a century in the same innings. India's total advances from 205–9 to 454 all out.

14

1835 Round-arm bowling is permitted for the first time – provided the ball is delivered from around shoulder height.

1872 Surrey dismiss MCC for 16 and beat them in a single day (Southerton 4–5, Marten 6–11). At one stage MCC lose seven wickets without scoring.

1935 Northants beat Somerset at Taunton, their last win for four years. In between they play 99 matches without victory.

1941 Birth of Nasim-ul-Ghani at Delhi. At 16 years 248 days he becomes the youngest Test cricketer on his début for Pakistan v West Indies, in the match in which Hanif Mohammad scores 337. Nasim's record later passes to Mushtaq Mohammad.

15

1899 Bill Howell, a bee farmer from New South Wales, takes 10–28 for the Australians v Surrey at The Oval. It is his first match in England.

1924 Glamorgan dismiss Lancashire for 49 at Aigburth, Liverpool and then are skittled for 22 (Cecil Parkin 6–6).

1935 Birth of Ted Dexter in Italy. Known as 'Lord Ted' for his imperious batting for Cambridge University, Sussex and England, he plays 62 times for England, captains the side and scores 4502 Test runs. A TV commentator and leading amateur golfer, in 1989 he becomes England's cricket supremo.

1948 Australia score 721 v Essex at Southend, the highest total in one day's first-class cricket.

1966 First day of Sunday play in County Championship – Essex v Somerset at Ilford.

MAY

16

1890   Arthur Shrewsbury and William Gunn complete their world-record partnership of 398 for Nottinghamshire's 2nd wicket v Sussex at Trent Bridge.

1955   Ray Lindwall (Australia), the greatest fast bowler of his day, scores his second Test century v West Indies at Bridgetown.

1956   Jim Laker (Surrey) takes all ten Australian wickets at The Oval (10–88). The same year he does it again in the Old Trafford Test.

Ray Lindwall – the batsman.

R.A. Garrett of John Player and S.C. Griffith, secretary of M.C.C., sign the contract for the sponsorship of the Sunday League to establish regular Sunday cricket.

MAY

Graham Dilley with protection against the sun in Australia.

17

1875   James Southerton takes 16–52 in one day's play for South v North at Lord's.

1888   Birth of 'Titch' Freeman at Lewisham. One of the game's great leg-break bowlers, the Kent spinner takes 100 wickets in a season 17 times and is the only man to pass 300. His first-class record is 3776 wickets at 18.42.

1895   W.G. Grace (Gloucestershire) completes his 100th first-class century v Somerset at Bristol, the first of 22 batsmen to reach this milestone.

1924   In an inter-divisional Ships' Shield match at Purfleet, Essex, J.W. Brockley clean-bowls all ten opposition batsmen in 11 balls, for two runs.

18

1886   Lancashire beat MCC at Lord's in one day, dismissing the home side for 30 and 92.

1905   Birth of Hedley Verity at Leeds. The Yorkshire and England left-arm spinner takes 15 Australian wickets for 104 at Lord's in 1934 in the game later

MAY

known as 'Verity's match'. Against Notts at Leeds he once takes 10–10.

1935   Harold Gimblett makes his brilliant début for Somerset v Essex at Frome. Coming in at 107–6 he hits 123 in 80 minutes, completing his century in 63 minutes.

1959   Birth of Graham Dilley at Dartford – the Kent, Worcestershire and England fast bowler.

E.M. Grace.

19

1874   Birth of Gilbert Jessop at Cheltenham. The Gloucestershire and England batsman becomes renowned for his ferocious hitting. He still holds the English record for the fastest Test century (75 minutes); his record for the fastest first-class century (40 minutes) lasts from 1897 to 1920 and his double century in 120 minutes (1903) remains a record until 1984–85.

1948   Bill Edrich (168*) and Denis Compton (252*) set an English record for their 3rd wicket stand of 424* for Middlesex v Somerset at Lord's.

1955   Denis Atkinson (219) and Cyril Depeiza (122) complete a world record stand of 347 for the 7th wicket for West Indies v Australia at Bridgetown.

20

1905   George Hirst hits the highest first-class innings by a Yorkshire player, scoring 341 v Leicestershire at Grace Road.

1911   Death of E.M. Grace at the age of 69. Brother of W.G., he was a doctor and fine all-round cricketer, scoring more than 10,000 first-class runs.

1911   Edwin Alletson (Notts) scores 189 in 90 minutes v Sussex at Hove, going from 50 to his final score in just 30 minutes.

1965   Hampshire dismiss Yorkshire for 23, their lowest first-class score, at Middlesborough. 'Butch' White takes 6 for 10, including a spell of 5–0.

MAY

21

1866 George Frederick Gracc, younger brother of W.G., makes his first-class début for Gentlemen of England v Oxford University at The Parks. Then aged 15 years 159 days, he is the third-youngest first-class cricketer in Britain (for youngest see 13 June).

1925 Somerset meet Lancashire for the first time since 1911. Somerset are dismissed for 73 and 74 and lose by nine wickets, all in a single day.

22

1826 Birth of George Parr at Radcliffe-on-Trent, Nottinghamshire. The first man to captain an England touring team (to Canada and United States in 1859), he scores 6626 first-class runs at 20.20 in an age when runs were much harder to come by.

1879 Birth of Warwick Armstrong at Kyneton, Victoria. The mighty all-rounder, 6ft 2in tall and weighing in excess of 19st, captains Australia on the whitewash tour of England in 1921, and in 50 Tests scores 2863 runs at 38.68 and takes 87 wickets at 33.59.

Albert Trott.

1907 Albert Trott (Middlesex) performs the rare feat of two hat-tricks in one innings, v Somerset at Lord's, finishing with 7–20 in eight overs. After the first hat-trick he takes another wicket with his next ball – four in four.

23

1899 A dubious benefit for Wilf Flowers. Middlesex play Somerset at Lord's in a match assigned to the benefit of the Notts and England player. The first day is washed out by rain, then Middlesex win in a single day. Despite being dismissed for 86, they limit Somerset to 44 and 35 (Albert Trott 11–31).

1918 Birth of D.C.S. Compton at Hendon. The most audaciously successful batsman in post-war England breaks many records though his best-remembered feats are achieved in 1947 when he scores 18

W. W. ARMSTRONG.

No 18
Issued with
MORRIS'S
High Grade Cigarettes.
A SERIES OF 25 SUBJECTS
·AUSTRALIAN·
CRICKETERS

W. W. Armstrong.

Australia regained the "Ashes" in 1920 when, under Armstrong's captaincy, the Australians won all five Tests against J. W. H. T. Douglas's team. Warwick Armstrong, a tall heavily-built player, probably one of the most massive cricketers ever born, made 2172 runs in Test matches, with the average of 35.03.

B MORRIS & SONS Ltd
LONDON, E.I

centuries and 3816 runs. He holds the CBE for services to cricket.

1969   It is announced that popular Northants and England opener Colin Milburn will lose his left eye following a late night car crash.

24

1877   Oxford University are dismissed by MCC Club & Ground at Cowley Marsh, Oxford for 12, the lowest innings in first-class cricket. Northants equal the record in 1907, and University supporters might claim the men in maroon fared worse than their team, as Oxford had to bat one man short.

1900   Johnny Briggs (Lancashire) takes all ten Worcestershire wickets for 55 runs at Old Trafford.

1923   Harry Howell becomes the first of three Warwickshire bowlers (Hollies and Bannister are the others) to take all ten wickets in an innings when he dismisses the Yorkshire batsmen (10–51) at Edgbaston.

1927   Yorkshire lose to Warwickshire at Hull, their first defeat in 71 matches, since August 1924, the longest unbeaten run in the County Championship.

25

1868   Australia's first side to visit Britain play their first match, v Surrey Gentlemen. The Australians are coached and captained by Charles Lawrence who had earlier played for Surrey and Middlesex.

1967   Sophia Gardens is officially opened as the new county ground of Glamorgan CCC.

1982   Graham Gooch hits a Benson & Hedges record score of 198* for Essex v Sussex at Hove, the visitors reaching 327 in their 55 overs.

1985   Allan Border (Australians) scores his fourth century of the tour v Derbyshire at Derby, the hundreds coming in successive matches.

Another century for Border in 1985, this time in the Fourth Test at Old Trafford.

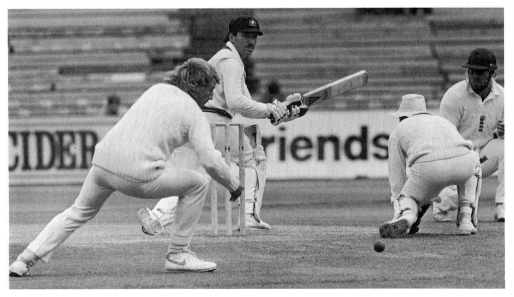

MAY

26

1871 Lancashire are routed by Derbyshire at Old Trafford, all out for 25 (Dove Gregory 6–9), their lowest-ever score.

1876 Birth of Percy Perrin in London. The Essex batsman hits a world-record 68 fours in an innings of 343* v Derbyshire at Chesterfield. In an extraordinary match Essex score 597 and 97 and lose to Derby (548 and 149 for 1) by nine wickets!

1884 In just four hours' play at Aston, Birmingham, the Australian tourists beat Eleven of England by four wickets. Chief damage is done by 'The Demon', F.R. Spofforth, who takes 7–34 and 7–3.

1947 Birth of Glenn Turner at Dunedin. New Zealand's greatest-ever batsman hits nearly 35,000 first-class runs, completing his 100th century for Worcestershire v Warwickshire in 1982 at Worcester and going on to make 311*, then the highest score recorded for the county.

27

1878 MCC are dismissed for 33 and 19 by the Australians at Lord's (F.R. Spofforth 11–20). The visitors reply with 41 and 12 for 1 to make a match aggregate of 105 runs, the lowest for a completed first-class match.

1931 'Titch' Freeman (Kent) takes all ten Lancashire wickets for 79 at Old Trafford, the third time he has achieved the feat.

1938 Don Bradman (Australia) scores his 1000th run of the season, the earliest date this has been done in the English season.

28

1880 Thirty-nine wickets fall in one day in the match between Oxford University and MCC at the Old Magdalen ground, Oxford, a first-class record.

1906 Tom Wass (Notts) takes 16–69 in a single day v Lancashire at Liverpool. Two years later he takes 16 Essex wickets at Trent Bridge, the only man to perform the feat twice.

1908 After making 356, Yorkshire dismiss Nottinghamshire for 17 and 15, winning by an innings and 341 runs. George Hirst returns match figures of 12–19.

1912 Australian bowler Jimmy Matthews takes two hat-tricks in the same Test, v South Africa at Old Trafford in a Triangular Tournament, the only time this has been done. They are also the only wickets he takes in the match.

1934 Jack Hobbs scores his 197th and final century for Surrey v Lancashire at Old Trafford, at the age of 51 years 163 days.

29

1902 The England team for the first Test v Australia contains 11 players who have made first-class centuries. This is the first Test match to be staged at Edgbaston. It ends in a draw.

1965 In the Edgbaston Test between England and New Zealand, it is so cold that the players have to be revived with hot drinks on two occasions.

1988 Graeme Hick (Worcs) completes 1000 runs before the end of May, v West Indies at Worcester, only the second man since the war to achieve the feat, the only one to do so with the aid of a quadruple century.

MAY

Derek Pringle watches Viv Richards on his way to the highest score in a one-day international.

30

1887   F. Lacey scores 323* for Hampshire v Norfolk at Southampton, the highest individual score in a Minor County match (Hampshire do not join the County Championship until 1895).

1895   W.G. Grace becomes the first to score 1000 runs in May, completing the feat in the space of 22 days.

1899   Bobby Abel completes his 357* for Surrey v Somerset at The Oval, the second highest innings in the County Championship at that time.

1902   Australia are dismissed for 36 by England at Edgbaston, their lowest innings in Test cricket (Rhodes 7–17).

1983   Surrey are dismissed by Essex for 14 at Chelmsford, their lowest-ever first-class score (Norbert Phillip 6–4). But Surrey save the match!

31

1934   Kent set two records with the highest total for the county of 803 for 4 and the highest innings for the county, Bill Ashdown's 332 begun the previous day. It all happens v Essex at Brentwood.

1950   In the Test trial at Bradford Jim Laker takes 8 for 2 in 14 overs (12 maidens). He is selected.

1984   Viv Richards scores 189* for West Indies v England at Old Trafford, the highest individual score in a one-day international.

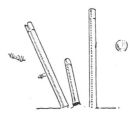

JUNE

Colin Milburn shows no respect for Wes Hall at Old Trafford.

1

1874   Alf Shaw (MCC) takes all ten wickets v North at Lord's, finishing with 10–73 in 36.2 overs.

1907   Colin Blythe (Kent) dismisses 17 Northamptonshire batsmen at Northampton for 48 runs, the best-ever Championship figures for most wickets and least runs conceded.

1928   Playing for Gloucestershire v Somerset at Bristol, P.T. Mills takes 5–0 in 6.4 overs.

1985   Viv Richards (Somerset) becomes the first West Indian to score 300 runs in one day, hitting 322 v Warwickshire at Taunton, with eight sixes and 42 fours. This is a new individual record for the county.

2

1914   Individual records set for two counties in separate matches. Sam Coe completes 252* for Leicestershire v Northants at Grace Road and Frank Foster hits 305* for Warwickshire v Worcestershire at Dudley.

1939   David Emrys Davies sets the Glamorgan record with 287* v Gloucestershire at Newport, again in the last season before a world war.

1966   Colin Milburn makes his Test début for England v West Indies at Old Trafford. Run out without scoring in the first innings, he hits back with 94 in the second.

3

1893   Frank Shacklock (Notts) takes 8–46 v Somerset, including four wickets in four balls.

1899   W.G. Grace makes his last Test appearance at the age of 50 years 320 days, v Australia at Trent Bridge. This makes him the oldest Test captain of all time.

1928   Birth of John Reid at Auckland. New Zealand's best captain of his generation, he scores over 3400 Test runs and takes 85 wickets, and takes the world record for most sixes in an innings (15).

4

1827   The inaugural Oxford v Cambridge Varsity match ends in a draw. The fixture is not fully established until 1851.

1957   In the final day of the first Test v West Indies at Edgbaston Colin Cowdrey (154) and Peter May (285*) take England's

4th wicket stand to 411, a Test record. May's innings is the highest by an England captain.

1964 Geoffrey Boycott makes his Test début v Australia at Trent Bridge. He makes 48, then fractures a finger in the field and does not bat in the second innings.

Early runs for Geoff Boycott at Trent Bridge at the beginning of his Test career.

1952 Fred Trueman makes his Test début for England v India at Headingley and helps to reduce the Indians to 0 for 4 in their second innings.

1964 Glamorgan score 134 for 3 in 95 overs v Hampshire, the lowest total for a full day's first-class play in Britain since 1864.

1971 Pakistan declare their first innings v England at Edgbaston on 608–7, their highest score v England until 1987 when they score 708 at The Oval.

JUNE

6

1874 Birth of George Harman, believed to be one of only four first-class cricketers to reach the age of 100. His first-class experience is limited to one match for Dublin University; he plays Rugby Union for Ireland on two occasions. He has a brother, William, also a first-class cricketer, who lives to the age of 93.

1912 Kent dismiss Leicestershire for 25 runs at Leicester, the home side's lowest first-class innings (C. Blythe 7–9).

1953 Lancashire beat Somerset in a single day at Bath by an innings and 24 runs. Played on a newly laid pitch, the match ends before six o'clock and is a financial disaster for all-rounder Bertie Buse, whose benefit match it is.

1957 Birth of Mike Gatting at Kingsbury. The Middlesex and England captain scores over 20,000 first-class runs.

7

1867 Sussex dismiss Kent at Gravesend for their lowest-ever total – 18 in 113 balls (Southerton 6–7). Only ten batted.

1899 Cyril Bland (Sussex) takes all ten Kent wickets for 48 at Tonbridge.

1957 Micky Stewart (Surrey) sets a first-class record for most catches by an outfielder in an innings when he catches seven Northants batsmen. He finishes the season with 77, one short of Walter Hammond's all-time record.

1970 Alan Ward (Derbyshire) takes four wickets in four balls in a John Player League game v Sussex at Derby.

Derek Underwood, a promising member of the Kent 2nd XI in 1963.

8

1925 Playing for Yorkshire v Middlesex, Percy Holmes scores 315*, the highest innings at Lord's, surpassing 278 by William Ward (MCC) in 1820. Holmes's record stands for one year only, beaten by Surrey's Jack Hobbs (316*).

1926 George Cox takes 17 Warwickshire wickets for 106 at Horsham, the best match return by a Sussex bowler.

1945 Birth of Derek Underwood at Bromley. The deceptive Kent and England bowler is one of the most respected players of the 1970s, taking 297 Test wickets at 25.83.

1950 Alf Valentine (West Indies) makes his Test début v England at Old Trafford and takes the first eight England wickets, the second player after A.E. Trott (1894–95) to take eight in one innings on his début.

JUNE

------------------- **9** -------------------

1906 Surrey's Thomas Hayward completes his fourth century in a week – 144* and 100 v Notts followed by 143 and 125 v Leicestershire.

1955 Ken Barrington (England) and Trevor Goddard (South Africa) make their Test débuts at Trent Bridge. Barrington launches his distinguished Test career with a duck.

1967 Geoffrey Boycott (England) makes his highest Test score, 246* v India at Headingley, but takes so long about it (573 minutes) that he is excluded from the next Test.

------------------- **10** -------------------

1864 Playing for MCC v Oxford University at Lord's, H.E. Bull is dismissed for hitting the ball twice, the first instance in first-class cricket.

1864 Over-arm bowling is legalised.

1938 Charlie Barnett (England) scores 98 before lunch v Australia at Trent Bridge, the highest total before lunch on the first day of a Test match. He reaches his century off the first ball after lunch.

------------------- -------------------

1896 A.D. Pougher (MCC) takes 5–0 in three overs v Australia at Lord's. The visitors are dismissed for 18 runs.

1907 Northants are dismissed for 12 by Gloucestershire at Gloucester, the lowest innings total in the County Championship.

1938 Denis Compton scores 102 for England v Australia at Trent Bridge and at 20 years 19 days becomes the youngest player to score a Test century for England.

1956 In the first county match to be played at Stroud Ken Smales (Notts) completes his demolition of the Gloucestershire batsmen by taking six wickets for an innings analysis of 10–66.

Denis Compton in his first Test innings against New Zealand in 1937.

JUNE

1896 J.T. Hearne (Middlesex) completes 100 wickets for the season, the earliest date this milestone has been reached.

1935 Alf Gover (Surrey) takes four Worcestershire wickets in four balls at Worcester.

1936 Charlie Parker (Gloucestershire) equals J.T. Hearne's feat of 1896.

1957 Birth of Javed Miandad at Karachi. The first Pakistani to play in more than 50 consecutive Test matches.

13

1867 Playing for Hampshire v Kent at Gravesend, Charles Robertson Young becomes the youngest person to play English first-class cricket. He is aged 15 years 131 days.

1905 Birth of K.S. Duleepsinhji at Sarodar. Nephew of the great Ranji, he plays for England in 12 Tests and scores 15,485 first-class runs at 49.95.

1935 Walter Hammond scores 116 for Gloucestershire v Somerset at Bristol, his 100th century.

1938 Stan McCabe scores a brilliant 232 for Australia v England at Trent Bridge. It takes him 235 minutes and represents 77% of the 300 Australian runs scored while he is at the crease.

14

1922 First day of the astounding match between Warwickshire and Hampshire at Birmingham. Warwickshire score 223 then bowl out Hampshire for 15. Following on, Hampshire score 521 and

dismiss Warwickshire for 158 to win by 155 runs.

1929 Birth of Alan Davidson in Lisarow, New South Wales. In the famous 'Tied Test' of 1960–61 the Australian all-rounder becomes the first man to score 100 runs and take 10 wickets in a Test match.

1961 Rudi Webster, in his début for Scotland at Greenock, dismisses Dickie Dodds (MCC) with his first ball. In the second innings he dismisses Arthur Phebey, again with his first ball.

1967 Alan Dixon (Kent) returns the best bowling figures in a Gillette Cup match, 7–15 v Surrey at The Oval.

1924 Maurice Tate (4–13 including a wicket with his first ball in Test cricket) and A.E.R. Gilligan (6–7) bowl out South Africa for 30 at Edgbaston.

1929 'Gubby' Allen (Middlesex) takes 10–40 v Lancashire at Lord's, including eight clean-bowled, the last time this occurred in a first-class match.

1960 The last County Championship match to be completed in one day. Kent score 187 v Worcestershire at Tunbridge Wells and bowl out the opposition for 25 and 61.

1927 Birth of Tom Graveney in Northumberland. Awarded the OBE for services to cricket, the stylish right-hander plays for Gloucestershire, Worcestershire and Queensland, scoring 47,793 first-class runs at 44.91.

JUNE

1932   Herbert Sutcliffe and Percy Holmes complete their record-breaking first-wicket partnership of 555 for Yorkshire v Essex at Leyton. The partnership lasts 7 hours 25 minutes and the record stands until 1976–77.

1958   Les Jackson (Derbyshire) performs a hat-trick v Worcestershire at Kidderminster; all three batsmen are caught by wicket-keeper George Dawkes.

The famous partnership of Holmes and Sutcliffe.

JUNE

1930 Copley's amazing catch turns the Trent Bridge Test. Sydney Copley, a member of the Notts groundstaff with no first-class experience, comes on as substitute fielder for Harold Larwood, takes a brilliant catch to dismiss Australia's Stan McCabe and puts England on course for victory. He goes on to play one first-class match in his career.

1935 Thomas Mitchell (Derbyshire) takes all ten Leicestershire wickets for 64 runs, finishing the innings in 19.1 overs.

1965 John Snow makes his Test début for England v New Zealand at Lord's in Fred Trueman's last Test.

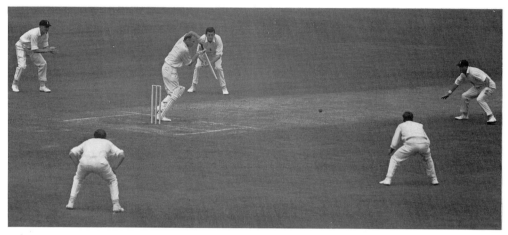

John Snow stands at short-leg as Fred Trueman bowls to New Zealand's F.J. Cameron at Lord's.

Kapil Dev to the rescue at Tunbridge Wells in 1983.

18

1863 The match at Lord's between MCC and Oxford University is completed in a single day, Oxford winning by an innings and 20 runs.

1874 Oxford University again win in a single day, beating Middlesex by an innings and 15 runs.

1894 Thomas Richardson (Surrey) takes all ten Essex wickets for 45 runs, then a record for the fewest balls (78) needed to perform the feat.

1895 Arthur Mold (Lancashire) takes 15–85 in a single day v Nottinghamshire at Trent Bridge as the home side are dismissed twice.

1983 Kapil Dev rescues India v Zimbabwe at Tunbridge Wells in the World Cup. India are on an embarrassing 17 for 5 when he goes in and scores 175* out of the winning total of 266 for 8.

19

1868 C.A. Absolom (Cambridge University) is dismissed v Surrey at The Oval for 'obstructing the field' – the first time this has happened in a first-class match.

1903 Birth of Walter Hammond at Dover. The great Gloucestershire and England leader is a prolific batsman with more than 50,000 runs to his credit and a deceptive medium-paced bowler who takes 732 wickets. His highest innings is 336* v New Zealand at Auckland in 1932–33.

1978 After scoring 108 in England's first innings v Pakistan at Lord's, Ian Botham takes 8–34, the first man to score a century and take eight wickets in the same Test.

1981 After 20 years of first-class cricket Bob Taylor, the Derbyshire and England wicket-keeper, makes his maiden century v Yorkshire.

20

1921 Two bowlers take ten wickets in an innings: Bill Bestwick (Derbyshire) takes 10–40 v Glamorgan at Cardiff, and John 'Farmer' White (Somerset) takes 10–76 v Worcestershire at Worcester. In the 1921 season this rare feat is performed five times.

1954 Birth of Allan Lamb at Cape Province. The Northants and England batsman wins his county cap in his début season, 1978, and is named a Wisden Cricketer of the Year in 1980.

1982 Raymond Illingworth is appointed captain of Yorkshire at the age of 50 years 15 days, the oldest player to be elected on a long-term basis.

Ray Illingworth back in Yorkshire colours.

JUNE

21

1872   Henry Phillips (Sussex) becomes the second wicket-keeper (after Edward Pooley) to claim ten victims in one match when he catches five and stumps five Surrey batsmen at The Oval.

1901   Yorkshire bowl out Nottinghamshire at Trent Bridge for their lowest-ever score, 13. Wilf Rhodes (6–4) and Schofield Haigh (4–8) are the destroyers.

1910   The Derbyshire pair John Chapman and Arnold Warren put on a world-record 283 for the 9th wicket v Warwickshire at Blackwell, raising their team's score from 131–8 to 414.

1913   Warwickshire are dismissed by Kent at Tonbridge for 13, their lowest first-class score. Blythe and Woolley each return figures of 5 for 6.

1975   West Indies beat Australia by 17 runs at Lord's to win the first Prudential World Cup. Clive Lloyd wins the Man of the Match award for his 102.

22

1814   The inaugural match on the present site of Lord's cricket ground. MCC beat Hertfordshire by an innings.

1886   W.G. Grace completes a remarkable all-round feat for MCC v Oxford University: after scoring 104 in his only innings he takes 10–49 in Oxford's second innings.

1988   Michael Holding establishes a world record for one-day cricket when he takes 8–21 for Derbyshire v Sussex at Hove in the NatWest Trophy.

Colin Cowdrey takes the catch which beat Walter Hammond's record.

23

1925   Middlesex, set a target of 500 to beat Nottinghamshire, at Trent Bridge, are struggling at 231–6 then Patsy Hendren and F.T. Mann take them to victory with a stand of 271* in 175 minutes. It is the only occasion a County Championship match has been won with a fourth innings score in excess of 500.

1934   Bertie Oldfield (Australia) becomes the first wicket-keeper to score 1000 runs and claim 100 victims in Test cricket.

1972   Australia's Bob Massie dismisses eight England batsmen on his Test début. At Lord's he takes 8–84 in 32.5 overs.

1979   West Indies win the second World Cup, beating England by 92 runs at Lord's.

24

1960   Geoff Griffin becomes the first South African to perform the hat-trick in Test cricket, v England at Lord's. His victims: Smith, Walker, Trueman.

1968   Colin Cowdrey catches Gleeson (Australia) at slip to take his 111th victim in Test cricket, beating Wally Hammond's record for an outfielder.

1974   England dismiss India at Lord's for 42, their lowest score in Test cricket. Old takes 5–21, Arnold 4–19.

25

1921   Charlie McCartney (Australia) hits the fastest triple century in England, v Notts at Trent Bridge, reaching his 300 in 205 minutes. He goes on to make 345, the most runs scored by an individual in a single day's play.

Geoff Arnold and Chris Old celebrate their destruction of India.

1934   Hedley Verity takes 14 Australian wickets at Lord's, the most in a day's play by one bowler in a Test match in England.

1938   Michael Harbottle scores 156 for the Army v Oxford University at Sandhurst. It is his only first-class innings, and the highest score by any batsman making just one first-class appearance in England.

1963   Colin Cowdrey returns to the field with his arm in plaster to stand at the bowler's end for the last two balls v West Indies at Lord's. Any one of four results is possible when he arrives at the crease; England hold out thanks to David Allen and the match is drawn.

1983   Kapil Dev leads India to a 43-run victory over the West Indies at Lord's to win the third World Cup.

JUNE

26

1745   The first women's cricket match is played between XI 'maids' of Bramley and XI of Hambledon at Gosden Common, near Guildford.

1871   Samuel Evan Butler takes 10–38 for Oxford University v Cambridge University, the only time a bowler has taken ten wickets in an innings in the Varsity match.

1935   Andy Sandham (Surrey) hits his 100th first-class century with 103 v Hampshire at Basingstoke.

1953   In the Test v Australia at Lord's, Alec Bedser becomes the first bowler to take 200 Test match wickets for England.

27

1896   Cambridge University beat MCC at Lord's by scoring 507–7 in their fourth innings. It is the highest fourth-innings score by a side winning a match in England.

1913   Tom Hayward (Surrey) completes his 100th first-class century v Lancashire at The Oval. He is the second man after W.G. Grace to reach this milestone.

1939   George Headley scores 107 for West Indies v England at Lord's after scoring 106 in the first innings. He is the first man to perform this feat at Lord's.

1949   Martin Donnelly scores 206 v England at Lord's, the only New Zealander to hit a double century v England in a Test match.

1984   Surrey's Nick Falkner and Keith Medlycott both score centuries on their first-class débuts v Cambridge University, the first time this has been done in the same match.

28

1899   Thirteen-year-old A.E.J. Collins scores a world-record 628* in a junior house match at Clifton School. His innings, spread over five afternoons, takes him 6 hours 50 minutes.

1906   George Hirst (Yorkshire) completes the double of 1000 runs and 100 wickets in the earliest time this has been achieved.

1926   Jack Hobbs, batting against Australia at Lord's, becomes the first player to score 4000 Test runs.

1969   John Hampshire scores a century on his Test début, v West Indies at Lord's.

29

1709   The first known cricket match between two counties takes place – Kent v Surrey at Dartford Brent.

1911   Robert Burrows (Worcestershire) bowls William Huddleston (Lancashire) at Old Trafford and one of the bails travels a record 67 yards 6 inches.

1903   Les Ames and Gubby Allen put on 246 for the England 8th wicket v New Zealand at Lord's, still a Test record for that wicket and the oldest Test partnership record still standing.

1950   West Indies win their first Test victory in England, at Lord's, by a margin of 326 runs.

30

1899   J.T. Hearne takes the first Test hat-trick in England, dismissing three notable Australian batsmen – Hill, Gregory and Noble – for nought apiece.

JUNE

1924   England score a Test record 503 runs in one day's play v South Africa at Lord's. Hobbs, Woolley, Sutcliffe and Hendren average 93 runs per hour for the loss of only two wickets.

1930   Australia declare at Lord's with a total of 726–6, their highest score v England. Bradman's 254 is his highest Test score at Lord's.

1981   Zaheer Abbas scores 1016 runs in the month of June, after bad weather has prevented him from batting in May.

John Hampshire is introduced to Prince Charles during the 1969 Lord's Test.

JULY

1

1902 Sussex pair K.S. Ranjitsinhji (230) and W. Newham (153) complete an English record partnership for the 7th wicket of 344, v Essex at Leyton.

1954 Khalid Hassan (Pakistan), aged 16 years 352 days, becomes the youngest-ever Test cricketer at the time, v England at Trent Bridge. It is the only Test he plays in.

1980 Twenty-two pupils of St Peter's School, Bournemouth complete a marathon cricket match. Beginning on 25th June, it lasts 5 days 17 hours non-stop.

2

1928 Gloucestershire hit their highest first-class score – 653–6 v Glamorgan at Bristol.

1951 Worcestershire 'keeper Hugo Yarnold dismisses seven Scotland batsmen at Dundee, stumping six of them – a world record.

1969 Ireland bowl out West Indies for 25 and defeat them by 9 wickets at Londonderry (O'Riordan 4–18, Goodwin 5–6).

3

1902 First day of the first and only Test match to be staged at Bramall Lane, Sheffield. Australia eventually beat England by 143 runs, C. Hill (119) scoring a unique Test century.

1911 Birth of Joe Hardstaff jnr at Nuncargate, Notts, also the birthplace of Harold Larwood. Like his father before him, Joe plays for his county and England, hitting 31,847 first-class runs at 44.35.

1951 Birth of Richard Hadlee at Christchurch, New Zealand. The most prolific wicket-taker in Test history, he passes Ian Botham's record total in 1988.

1984 Gordon Greenidge scores the first West Indian double century at Lord's, 214* v England in 300 minutes; and at Hastings Derek Underwood scores his first century for Kent, after 22 years and 618 innings.

Another highlight in Derek Underwood's career as a batsman – he top-scores with 30 in England's second innings against Australia at Brisbane in 1974.

4

1904 Walter Brearley (Lancashire) takes his 17th wicket of the match v Somerset at Old Trafford; his haul includes four wickets in four balls.

JULY

5

1981   Clive Rice scores 105* for Notts v Hampshire at Bournemouth, but his team are dismissed for 143, the lowest completed first-class innings in England to contain a century.

1984   In their NatWest match v Oxfordshire at Edgbaston, Warwickshire hit a competition record score of 392–5 (Kallicharran 206, also a record, and 6–32).

1988   The 144th Varsity match is washed out without a ball being bowled – for the first time in the history of the fixture.

1906   Tom Hayward (Surrey) scores his 2000th run of the season, the earliest date this target has been reached in the English season.

1929   Birth of Tony Lock at Limpsfield, Surrey. The controversial left-armer, also a brilliant close fielder, twice takes 200 first-class wickets in a season and his aggregate of 831 first-class catches is bettered only by Frank Woolley and W.G. Grace.

1954   Khalid Hassan (Pakistan) completes his Test career at the age of 16 years 356 days.

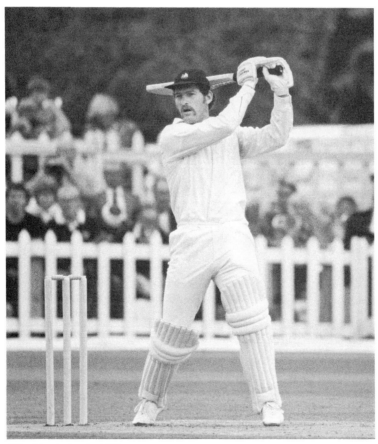

Clive Rice during the 1981 season.

JULY

6

1870 Birth of Andy Sandham at Streatham. The Surrey and England batsman sets a Test record v West Indies at Kingston in 1929–30 when he scores 325. His career total of first-class runs is 41,284 (at 44.82).

1927 Ian Peebles (later of Middlesex and England) makes his first-class début for Gentlemen v Players. The 19-year-old Scot's first wicket is that of Andy Sandham. He goes on to claim a career total of 923 then becomes a successful cricket writer.

1988 John O'Brien (Cheshire) becomes the first non-first-class bowler to take a hat-trick in a Gillette/NatWest match; his victims are Derbyshire.

7

1868 Edward Pooley (Surrey) claims a record 12 victims in a match by a wicket-keeper. At The Oval he catches eight Sussex batsmen and stumps four.

1909 Frank Woolley and Arthur Fielder put on 235 for Kent's 10th wicket v Worcestershire at Stourbridge – an English last-wicket record.

1961 A.J.G. Pearson (Cambridge University) takes all ten Leicestershire wickets for 78 runs at Loughborough, the second Cambridge player to perform this feat after S.M.J. Woods in 1890. Pearson's captain in the match is Mike Brearley.

1987 Brothers Alan (140*) and Colin (161*) Wells of Sussex add 303* v Kent at Hove and save the match.

Andy Sandham batting for Surrey Against Kent in 1936.

JULY

Frank Woolley in the nets in 1937.

Ian Botham and Allan Lamb enjoy their partnership at The Oval.

1982 Ian Botham joins Allan Lamb for England v India at The Oval, with the score at 180–3. By close of play they add 144 in 28 overs, and Botham goes on to complete the fastest Test double century in terms of balls bowled – he needs 220 deliveries.

1932 Herbert Sutcliffe (132) scores his 100th first-class century, for Yorkshire v Gloucestershire at Bradford.

1957 Gami Goonesena scores 211 in the Varsity match, the highest-ever score for Cambridge in this series.

1906 Kent fast bowler Arthur Fielder takes 10–90 for Players v Gentlemen at Lord's, the only bowler to take all ten wickets in this fixture.

1976 England are dismissed for 71 v West Indies at Old Trafford (M. Holding 5–17), the lowest innings total in matches between the two countries.

1965 John Edrich completes his 310* for England v New Zealand at Headingley, the last time a Test triple century is scored in England.

JULY

Ravi Shastri congratulates Sunil Gavaskar after he scores his first century at Lord's during the MCC Bicentenary match.

Tony Lock, the destroyer of Kent in 1956.

1879 Derbyshire are dismissed for 16 by Nottinghamshire (Fred Morley 7–7), their lowest first-class total.

1884 The first day's play in the first Test match at Old Trafford is washed out by rain.

1949 Birth of Sunil Gavaskar at Bombay. In 1987 he becomes the first man to pass 10,000 Test runs, going on to hit 10,122 at 51.12.

1956 Tony Lock (Surrey) takes 10–54 v Kent at Blackheath; in his two matches against Kent that summer he totals 26–143.

1848 Edmund Hinkly (Kent) dismisses all ten England batsmen at Lord's. He is the first man known to perform this feat in first-class cricket

1913 Lancashire's Harry Dean takes 17 Yorkshire wickets for 91 runs (9–62 and 8–29) at Liverpool. It is the ninth best first-class match return of all time.

1930 Don Bradman scores a record 309 in one day's play v England at Headingley, going on to make 334 out of Australia's first-innings total of 566. He reaches 200 in 214 minutes, the fastest-ever Test double century.

12

1932   Hedley Verity takes 10–10 v Notts at Leeds, the best bowling figures ever in first-class cricket; full analysis 19.4 overs, 16 maidens, 10 runs, 10 wickets.

1950   Lancashire beat Sussex by an innings and 87 runs in a single day's play at Old Trafford. Thirty wickets fall for 391 runs.

1975   Derbyshire wicket-keeper Bob Taylor catches seven Yorkshire batsmen in an innings at Chesterfield – the second time he has performed the feat, which equals the English record.

1977   John Edrich (Surrey) scores his 100th century, v Derbyshire at The Oval, the fourth Surrey player to do so after Hobbs, Hayward and Sandham.

13

1747   Women cricketers play for the first time at a major venue, the Honourable Artillery Ground, London. Taking part are the 'maids' of Westdean, Chilgrove and Charlton.

1869   Charles Thornton (Kent) hits nine sixes v Sussex at The Common, Tunbridge Wells. At the time a six has to be hit out of the ground to count, not merely clear the boundary.

1976   Brian Close (England) plays in his final Test match, v West Indies at Old Trafford, at the age of 45 years 140 days.

14

1873   Lancashire opening bat A.N. Hornby scores 20 out of his side's total of 100 v Surrey at The Oval, including one stroke off James Street from which he runs 10.

1933   Hedley Verity (Yorkshire) bowls out Essex twice in a day at Leyton, taking 8–47 and 9–44.

1988   Chris Cowdrey becomes the latest son to captain his country after his father (Colin), when he is appointed captain of England for the Headingley Test v West Indies.

15

1822   The first known exponent of round-arm bowling, Kent's John Willes, is no-balled for throwing v MCC at Lord's. In disgust he mounts a horse and rides out of the ground, never to play cricket again.

1850   John Wisden clean-bowls all ten batsmen in an innings, the only time this has been done in a first-class match. The founder of the *Wisden Cricketers' Almanack* is playing for North v South at Lord's.

1902   K.S. Ranjitsinhji (Sussex) scores 180 before lunch v Surrey at Hastings, the highest score made in England during the pre-lunch session.

1924   A. Young of Somerset (198) is the only man to score a century when his county compile their highest first-class score, declaring on 675–9 v Hampshire at Bath.

1938   Arthur Fagg (Kent) completes a remarkable performance v Essex at Colchester, scoring a double century in each innings, the only time this has happened in first-class cricket. His scores: 244 and 202*.

JULY

Len Hutton is congratulated by Norman Yardley after scoring his 100th century. On the left is Don Brennan and on the right, Willie Watson.

16

1895   Archie MacLaren (Lancashire) completes his 424 v Somerset at Taunton, the biggest innings in the history of the County Championship.

1910   Birth of Stan McCabe at Grenfell, New South Wales. During the Bodyline series he plays one of Test cricket's great innings, defying the England pace attack at Sydney to score 187* in four hours.

1951   Master batsman Len Hutton scores the 100th century of his career, for Yorkshire v Surrey at The Oval.

17

1893   Batting against Australia at Lord's, Arthur Shrewsbury becomes the first man to score 1000 runs in Test cricket.

1903   After winning the toss and electing to bat against Yorkshire at Huddersfield, Worcestershire are bowled out for their lowest score, 24 (Hirst 5–18, Rhodes 5–4).

1983   Graham Gooch hits a John Player League record 176 for Essex v Glamorgan at Southend and Essex amass 310–5 in their 40 overs.

JULY

18

Two eminent cricketers share this birthday, both famous for their fierce enthusiasm and facial hair:

1848 W.G. Grace is born at Downend, Bristol, and in **1949** Dennis Lillee is born at Perth, Western Australia.

1896 George Giffen ('the W.G. Grace of Australia') becomes the first player to achieve the Test double of 1000 runs and 100 wickets.

1972 Mike Procter (Gloucestershire) performs the hat-trick v Essex at Westcliff, and in the match also scores a century. He finishes with bowling figures of 8–73 and scores of 51 and 102. Seven years later he repeats the rare hat-trick plus century feat v Leicestershire.

19

1894 Yorkshire beat Somerset by an innings and five runs in one day's play at Huddersfield. In their previous match, just across the Pennines v Lancashire, Somerset suffered a similar fate.

1904 Percy Perrin completes his 343* for Essex v Derbyshire at Chesterfield, a record score for the county.

1952 India suffer the distinction of being the only Test side to be dismissed twice in one day. At Old Trafford they are bowled out by England for 58 (Trueman 8–31) and 82 (A.V. Bedser 5–27, Lock 4–36).

20

1849 The War of the Roses begins with the first Yorkshire v Lancashire battle at Hyde Park, Sheffield.

1942 Barbados dismiss Trinidad for 16 runs in 69 minutes, the lowest first-class innings in the West Indies. Chief wicket-taker is Derek Sealy (8–8).

1981 In the Headingley Test, Ian Botham comes to the wicket with England on 135–7 in their second innings, still 92 behind Australia's first-innings score. By the close Botham is on 145*, having added 110 for the 8th wicket with Dilley (56) and 67 for the 9th with Old. Next day Bob Willis takes 8–43 and England win a famous victory.

The end of a remarkable Test match at Headingley, 1981.

JULY

21

1884 First day of first Test match at Lord's. England go on to beat Australia by an innings and five runs, and the first Test century on the ground is scored by England's A.G. Steel (148).

1899 In a gallant Army partnership, Major Wynard and Major Poore put on 411 for Hampshire and the county registers its highest score, 672–7, v Somerset at Taunton.

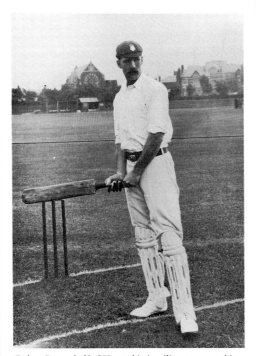

Robert Poore, half of Hampshire's military partnership.

1945 Birth of Barry Richards at Durban, South Africa. He plays county cricket for Gloucestershire (1 innings) and Hampshire (342 innings), hitting 28,358 runs in all first-class cricket at 54.74.

1964 Arnold Long (Surrey) sets a world wicket-keeping record v Sussex at Hove when he takes his 11th catch in the match.

22

1859 V.E. Walker Day. Playing for England v Surrey at The Oval, he takes 10–74 and also scores a century in the match. On the sixth anniversary of his ten-wicket feat, Walker repeats it for Middlesex v Lancashire at Old Trafford (10–104) and becomes the first man to take all ten twice.

1914 S.G. Smith (Northants) takes four wickets in four balls v Warwickshire at Edgbaston.

1935 Birth of Tom Cartwright at Coventry. The medium-pacer, renowned for his steadiness and skill, spends most of his career with Warwickshire and has later spells at Somerset and Glamorgan. He takes 1536 first-class wickets at 19.11.

Arnold Long, who established his record at the expense of the county he was later to captain.

23

1934 Don Bradman completes his innings of 304 v England at Headingley. It is the Australian's second triple century in successive Tests on this ground and he is the only batsman to score two in Test cricket.

1942 While playing for Sussex Home Guard v Surrey Home Guard at Lord's, Andy Ducat collapses and dies, aged 56. A dual soccer and cricket international, he played cricket for Surrey and soccer for Aston Villa, Southend, Arsenal and Fulham.

1949 Brian Close makes his England début v New Zealand at Old Trafford. At 18 years 149 days he becomes the youngest-ever England Test cricketer.

1953 Birth of Graham Gooch at Leytonstone. The Essex opener and county captain to date averages 42.74 at first-class level and 37.11 in Tests.

24

1902 At Old Trafford Victor Trumper (Australia) becomes the first of only four men to score a century before lunch on the first day of a Test match.

1929 'Tich' Freeman of Kent takes all ten Lancashire wickets for 131 at Maidstone, the first of the record three times he performs the feat.

1931 George Gunn (Notts) takes his overnight score to 183 v Warwickshire at Edgbaston. Later in the day his son George Vernon Gunn scores 100* – the only instance of father and son scoring centuries in the same first-class match.

The last appearance of 'W.G.'.

25

1900 For the second day running, and in the same match, Gilbert Jessop hits a century before lunch for Gloucestershire v Yorkshire at Bradford Park Avenue.

1900 Surrey score 270–0 in their fourth innings v Kent at The Oval – the highest fourth-innings total without loss in Britain.

1914 W.G. Grace plays his last game of cricket. At the age of 66 he turns out for Eltham v Grove Park and scores 69*.

1964 Bobby Simpson (Australia) completes his 311 v England at Old Trafford, the second-highest Test score in England and the highest first-class score on the ground.

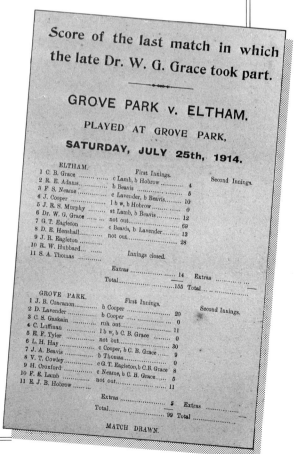

Score of the last match in which the late Dr. W. G. Grace took part.

GROVE PARK v. ELTHAM.

PLAYED AT GROVE PARK,

SATURDAY, JULY 25th, 1914.

ELTHAM.

	First Innings.		Second Innings.
1 C. B. Grace	c Lamb, b Hobrow		
2 R. E. Adams	b Beavis	4	
3 F. S. Neame	c Lavender, b Beavis	5	
4 J. Cooper	l b w, b Hobrow	10	
5 J. R. S. Murphy	st Lamb, b Beavis	0	
6 Dr. W. G. Grace	not out	12	
7 G. T. Eagleton		69	
8 D. E. Henshall	c Beavis, b Lavender	13	
9 J. R. Eagleton	not out	28	
10 R. W. Hubbard			
11 S. A. Thomas	Innings closed.		

Extras 14   Extras

Total 155   Total

GROVE PARK.

	First Innings.		Second Innings.
1 J. B. Concanon	b Cooper		
2 D. Lavender	b Cooper	20	
3 C. S. Gaskain	run out	0	
4 C. Luffman	l b w, b C. B. Grace	11	
5 E. F. Tyler	not out	0	
6 L. H. Hay	c Cooper, b C. B. Grace	30	
7 J. A. Beavis	b Thomas	9	
8 V. T. Cowley	c G. T. Eagleton, b C.B. Grace	0	
9 H. Croxford	c Neame, b C. B. Grace	8	
10 F. E. Lamb	not out	5	
11 E. J. B. Hobrow		11	

Extras 5   Extras

Total 99   Total

MATCH DRAWN.

JULY

26

1858   Birth in Wollongong of Thomas Garrett, Australian opening bowler in the first Test match at Melbourne, 1877.

1955   Trevor Bailey goes a record 79 minutes without adding to his score while playing for England v South Africa at Headingley.

1961   Tony Brown equals Micky Stewart's world record of seven catches in an innings by an outfielder, playing for Gloucestershire v Notts at Trent Bridge.

1984   Old Trafford celebrates its centenary of Test cricket when it stages the 4th Test against the West Indies.

27

1928   'Titch' Freeman takes his 200th wicket of the season, the earliest date this has been achieved in an English season.

1957   Godfrey Evans catches West Indian Collie Smith at Headingley and becomes the first wicket-keeper to claim 200 Test victims.

1969   After his allotted eight overs Brian Langford (Somerset) returns figures of 0–0 in a John Player League match v Essex at Yeovil, the most economical bowling in the history of the competition.

1974   John Jameson (240*) and Rohan Kanhai (213*) compile a world-record 2nd-wicket stand of 465 for Warwickshire v Gloucestershire at Edgbaston.

1985   Playing for Essex v Somerset at Taunton, David East equals Wally Grout's world record of eight victims in an innings by a 'keeper.

28

1936   Birth of Garfield Sobers at Barbados. The most outstanding all-rounder of his day, he scores 8032 Test runs, takes 235 wickets and 109 catches and hits the record Test score of 365*.

1937   Two batsmen perform the rare feat of scoring 300 runs in one day's play: Eddie Paynter hits 322 for Lancashire v Sussex at Hove and Richard Moore scores 316 for Hampshire v Warwickshire at Bournemouth.

1969   Ken Suttle plays his 423rd consecutive Championship game for Sussex, a first-class record in Britain, after a run beginning on 18th August 1954.

1982   Warwickshire's Alvin Kallicharran and Geoff Humpage put on 470 v Lancashire at Southport, a new English record for the 4th wicket, but the visitors lose the match by 10 wickets. In reply to Warwickshire's 523, Lancashire make 414–6 dec, bowl the opposition out for 111 and score 226–0 to win.

29

1897   Gilbert Jessop scores a century in 40 minutes for Gloucestershire v Yorkshire at Harrogate, the fastest first-class century before Percy Fender's 35-minute ton in 1920.

1927   C.P. Mead (Hampshire) scores his 100th first-class century v Northants, the fourth man to reach this milestone.

1986   Dennis Amiss (Warwickshire) becomes the 21st player to score 100 first-class centuries, hitting 101* v Lancashire at Edgbaston.

The scoreboard registers Dennis Amiss's 100th century.

3 1

1899 Playing for MCC Club and Ground v Australians at Lord's, Albert Trott hits a ball from Montague Noble over the Pavilion, a stroke that still waits to be emulated.

1943 Death of Hedley Verity in Caserta from injuries received in battle, aged 38. The Yorkshire and England bowler holds the record for the best first-class analysis (10–10) and in his career took 1956 first-class wickets at 14.90.

1956 Jim Laker dismisses Australia's Len Maddocks and completes the most remarkable piece of bowling in Test history, claiming 19 wickets in the Old Trafford Test.

1973 Lancashire's Frank Hayes scores a century on his England début v West Indies at The Oval. He is the latest Englishman to achieve this feat.

3 0

1921 Charlie Parker (Gloucestershire) takes 10–79 in 40.3 overs on the first day of the match v Somerset at Bristol.

1951 Peter May scores 138 on his Test début for England v South Africa at Headingley.

1982 Lancashire's Graeme Fowler completes the record of scoring a century in each innings, and in both needing the aid of a runner. The match is against Warwickshire at Southport.

The full story of Jim Laker's great achievement.

ENGLAND v. AUSTRALIA
AT OLD TRAFFORD
JULY 26, 27, 28, 30, 31, 1956

AUGUST

1

1866   W.G. Grace wins the 440 yards hurdles title at the first National Olympian Association meeting at Crystal Palace. The previous day he completed an innings of 224* for England v Surrey at The Oval.

1884   Alfred Shaw (Nottinghamshire) completes a hat-trick in the second innings v Gloucestershire at Trent Bridge. Having performed the same feat in the first innings, he becomes the first of only seven men to take a hat-trick twice in the same match.

1924   Frank Worrell, future West Indian captain, to be knighted for his services to cricket, is born at St Michael, Barbados.

1961   Richie Benaud's spell of 6–70 v England at Old Trafford brings Australia victory by 54 runs and with it retention of the Ashes.

2

1888   Surrey defeat Lancashire by an innings and 25 runs in a single day's play (George Lohmann 13–51).

1893   The match between the Australians and Oxford & Cambridge Universities Past and Present at Portsmouth ends with eight of the Australian batsmen contributing half-centuries towards their side's total of 843, the highest number of 50s in a first-class innings.

1898   Derbyshire hit 645 v Hampshire at Derby, their highest first-class score.

1981   Part 2 in the saga of 'Botham's Ashes'. At Edgbaston Australia, needing 142 to win, are 105 for 4. Botham then takes 5 for 1 off 28 balls, and Australia are all out for 121 (Botham 14–9–11–5).

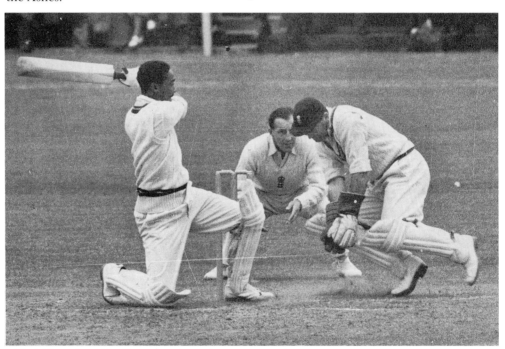

Bill Edrich watches and Godfrey Evans takes evasive action as Frank Worrell hits out at Old Trafford in 1950.

AUGUST

3

1907   Francis Tarrant (Middlesex) dismisses four Gloucestershire batsmen off four successive balls at Bristol, finishing with 9-41. He is the second Middlesex bowler that year to perform the feat, after Alfred Trott.

1978   The TCCB announce that a batsman cannot be caught off a rebound from his protective helmet – the first mention of helmets in cricket legislation.

1979   Gloucestershire beat Leicestershire to record their first win in a Championship match at Bristol for three years. Their star is Mike Procter who on the final day scores 122 and takes 7–26 including a hat-trick.

4

1896   W.G. Grace becomes the first man to score three triple centuries when he hits 301 for Gloucestershire v Sussex at Bristol; he is aged 48.

1947   Somerset are dismissed by Gloucestershire at Bristol for 25, their lowest first-class score (Tom Goddard 5–4).

1976   England's women's XI beat Australia by 8 wickets in the first women's match to be played at Lord's.

5

1933   Ted Bowley and John Langridge (Sussex) put on 490 for the 1st wicket v Middlesex at Hove, a Sussex record.

1949   Gloucestershire bowler Ken Graveney (elder brother of Tom) takes all ten Derbyshire wickets at Chesterfield. His figures are 10–66 in 18.4 overs.

Ken Graveney, senior member of a great Gloucestershire family.

1964   Tom Graveney scores the 100th century of his career, for Worcestershire v Northants at Worcester.

6

1900   Albert Trott (Middlesex) takes all ten Somerset wickets for 42 runs at Taunton, performing the feat in 14.2 overs.

1953   Birth of Iqbal Qasim at Karachi. In his eight-year Test career for Pakistan he takes 137 wickets.

1960   Hubert Preston, editor of *Wisden* from 1944 to 1951, dies at the age of 91. A soccer and cricket reporter for most of his life, he helped in the preparation of the *Cricketers' Almanack* from 1895 until promoted to editor.

AUGUST

1872   Playing for South v North at Canterbury, James Lillywhite jnr takes 10–129.

1947   Coming in at No.11 for Essex, Peter Smith hits 163 v Derbyshire at Chesterfield, the highest score by a No.11 in first-class cricket. His stand of 218 with Frank Vigar is the county record for the 10th wicket.

1948   Birth of Greg Chappell at Adelaide. The Australian captain plays in 87 Tests and averages 53.86 with the bat. Among his many records he hits 247* and 133 in one match v New Zealand in 1973–74, the most runs by one player in a Test.

1873   W.G. Grace takes 10–92 for the Gentlemen of Kent v MCC at Canterbury.

1909   Birth of Bill Voce at Annesley Woodhouse, Nottinghamshire. Best known as Harold Larwood's partner in the Bodyline series, he takes 98 Test wickets in his career at 27.88.

1956   Tom Graveney comes to the wicket for Gloucestershire v Glamorgan at Newport with the score at 9–2. He scores 200 out of his side's total of 298, the lowest completed innings to contain a double century.

1987   Pakistan complete their highest Test total, 708 v England at The Oval. Top scorers are Javed Miandad (260), Imran Khan (112) and Salim Malik (102).

1892   Lancashire defeat Somerset by eight wickets in a single day's play. Only two men take the wickets – Briggs (12) and Mold (8).

1976   Clive Lloyd equals Gilbert Jessop's record for the fastest double century. Playing for West Indians v Glamorgan at Swansea he scores 200 in exactly two hours – including a break for drinks.

1977   Chris Old completes a century in 37 minutes for Yorkshire v Warwickshire at Edgbaston, then the second fastest in first-class cricket.

1983   Middlesex hit the highest second innings score in county cricket – 634–7 v Essex.

1922   Charlie Parker (Gloucestershire) hits the wicket with five successive deliveries v Yorkshire at Bristol, but is denied a world record because the second hit is a no-ball.

1967   Alan Knott, statistically England's finest wicket-keeper/batsman – challenged only by Les Ames – makes his Test début v Pakistan at Trent Bridge. He does not concede a bye but, like many Test 'greats', begins his batting career with a duck.

1976   Death of Australian wicket-keeper Bert Oldfield at the age of 81. After Rodney Marsh and Wally Grout he is his country's top wicket-keeper with 130 Test dismissals; his 31 stumpings against England is a record in the history of the series.

1869   W.G. Grace hits 116* before lunch for MCC v Kent at Canterbury, the first player to score a century before lunch on the first day of a first-class match.

1896   George Davidson completes his innings of 274 for Derbyshire v

Alan Knott catches Ibadulla off Ken Higgs to record his first Test victim.

Lancashire at Old Trafford, the highest individual score for the county.

1950   Les Ames scores 131 for Kent v Middlesex at Canterbury and becomes the first and only wicket-keeper to complete 100 first-class centuries.

1951   Essex No.11 L.C.S. Jerman hits his first ball in first-class cricket for six, v Surrey.

1977   Geoffrey Boycott completes his 100th first-class century playing for England v Australia at Headingley.

AUGUST

12

1795 The first lbw decision is recorded when Surrey bowler Wells dismisses Hon. John Tufton (XIII of England) at Moulsey Hurst.

1876 W.G. Grace sets a new first-class record with 344 for MCC v Kent at Canterbury. A week later he scores 318* v Yorkshire.

1884 William Murdoch hits the first Test double century, 211 for Australia v England at The Oval.

1924 Birth of Derek Shackleton at Todmorden, Lancashire. The Hampshire medium-pacer holds the record for taking 100 wickets in 20 consecutive seasons (1949–68).

13

1902 Gilbert Jessop hits a century v Australia at The Oval in 75 minutes, the fastest Test century by an England batsman.

1912 Sydney Barnes takes 8–29 for England v South Africa at The Oval, the best figures in any Test on that ground.

1976 West Indies declare at 687–8 v England at The Oval, their highest score against England. Viv Richards's 291 is the highest by a West Indian against England in England.

1982 Mohsin Khan scores 200 for Pakistan v England at Lord's, the first Test double century at Lord's since Martin Donnelly's 206 for New Zealand in 1949.

Mohsin Khan is congratulated by Ian Botham after passing 200.

1873 In just 45 minutes and 82 balls Sussex are dismissed by Nottinghamshire at Hove for 19, their lowest-ever first-class total. Only ten batted.

1930 A.P. 'Titch' Freeman takes all ten Essex wickets for 53 runs at Southend. Between 1929 and 1931 he performs the all-ten feat once a season.

1948 Don Bradman goes to the wicket in his final Test at The Oval needing four runs to give him a Test average of 100.00. Eric Hollies dismisses him second ball and he has to settle for 99.94.

Celebration as Fred Trueman takes his 300th Test wicket.

1901 Yorkshire dismiss Essex at Leyton for 30, their lowest first-class total. This is the highest lowest total among the first-class counties.

1929 George Geary (Leicestershire) takes 10–18 v Glamorgan at Pontypridd, then the best-ever first-class bowling analysis.

1964 Fred Trueman takes his 300th Test victim v Australia at The Oval, the first bowler to reach this milestone.

1972 Pat Pocock (Surrey) becomes the last man to take four wickets in four balls. Playing against Sussex at Eastbourne he goes on to take five wickets in the over, six in nine balls and seven in 11 balls; up till then his analysis is less impressive – 0 for 63.

1981 Part 3 in the saga of 'Botham's Ashes'. At Old Trafford, England are only 101 ahead in their second innings at 104–5 when he comes in to bat. He hits 118 in 123 minutes with six sixes (Ashes record) and 13 fours, and sets up a victory by 103 runs.

1860 Birth of Lord Hawke at Gainsborough, Lincolnshire. He captains Yorkshire for 28 seasons (1883–1910), is county president (1898–1938), plays in five Tests for England and becomes president of the MCC.

1921 Warwick Armstrong, Australia's captain, protests at having to play Tests in three days by standing in the outfield reading a newspaper.

1950 Birth of Jeff Thomson at Sydney. The scourge of English batsmen in the mid-Seventies, together with Dennis Lillee, he takes 200 Test wickets at 28.00.

AUGUST

T. G. EVANS, C.B.E.

Cricketers of Kent No. 18

T. G. EVANS, C.B.E.

An England wicket-keeper of legendary fame (with 91 caps), and one of an illustrious Kentish line. A dangerous batsman who 4 times topped 1000 runs.

B Finchley, 1920. Kent 1939-67. England (91). rh batsman-wicket-keeper. 14882 runs, hs 144, av 21.22, 7 100s. c 816, st 250. In Tests, 2439 runs, hs 104, av 20.49, 2 100s. c 173, st 46.

Issued by
Kent County Cricket Club
*Sponsored by
E. C. Wharton-Tigar*

17

1928   Walter Hammond takes 10 catches in one match, a record for an outfielder. Playing for Gloucestershire v Surrey at Cheltenham, he also scores a century in each innings (139 and 143).

1946   Godfrey Evans makes his Test début v India at The Oval, and does not concede a bye in an innings of 331.

1976   Michael Holding completes figures of 14–149 v England at The Oval, the best match return by a West Indian bowler in Test cricket.

18

1925   After equalling W.G. Grace's record of 126 first-class centuries in Surrey's first innings v Somerset at Taunton, Jack Hobbs goes one better in the second innings, scoring 101*.

1934   Australia's Bill Ponsford and Don Bradman put on a Test record stand of 451 for the 2nd wicket v England at The Oval.

1955   Derek Shackleton (Hampshire) returns 8–4 in 11.1 overs v Somerset at Weston-super-Mare, one of the best innings analyses ever. In the second innings he takes 6–25.

John Brown and John Tunnicliffe with the Yorkshire team of 1903.

19

1898 John Brown and John Tunnicliffe put on a world-record 554 for Yorkshire's 1st wicket v Derbyshire at Chesterfield.

1919 Playing in his benefit match for Surrey v Kent at The Oval, Jack Hobbs is joined by J.N. Crawford in a remarkable partnership: set 95 to win in 42 minutes, they hit the runs with ten minutes to spare.

PLAYER'S CIGARETTES

W. R. HAMMOND (GLOUCESTERSHIRE)

CRICKETERS, 1934
A SERIES OF 50
11
W. R. HAMMOND
(Gloucestershire and England)
For ten seasons Walter Hammond has ranked among our greatest batsmen and fieldsmen with medium-paced bowling completing his equipment. Of very powerful build, Hammond drives tremendously hard. When first visiting Australia in 1928 he created a record by scoring 905 (average 113) in the five Tests, but Bradman has since beaten this record. Unsurpassed in getting 251 and 200 in consecutive innings in the Tests at Sydney and Melbourne, 1928-9, he followed up with 119 not out and 177 in the Fourth Test at Adelaide. In 1927 he scored 1,000 runs in May, and in 1933 headed the batting figures with 3,323 runs, average 67.
ISSUED BY
JOHN PLAYER & SONS
BRANCH OF THE IMPERIAL TOBACCO CO.
(OF GREAT BRITAIN & IRELAND), LTD.

1946 Walter Hammond becomes the first to score 7000 Test runs, batting v India at The Oval.

1985 Tim Robinson and David Gower complete a stand of 331 for England's 2nd wicket v Australia at Edgbaston, the second highest partnership for England v Australia for any wicket.

20

1900 Devon County Wanderers win the Olympic gold medal for Great Britain, beating France by 158 runs.

1929 Herbert Sutcliffe completes his second century v South Africa at The Oval, the second time he has performed the feat.

1935 Les Ames scores 123 before lunch for England v South Africa at The Oval, the highest score made before lunch in a Test match.

PLAYER'S CIGARETTES

L. E. G. AMES (KENT)

CRICKETERS, 1934
A SERIES OF 50
1
L. E. G. AMES
(Kent and England)
Leslie Ames started strongly in 1927 when scoring 1,036 in his first full season for Kent, and has become an England batsman in addition to keeping wicket in all the Tests in the 1932-3 Australian tour. Last season he was sixth in the country's aggregates with 3,058, average 58·80. Of his eight centuries three were over 200, including 295, his highest innings, and two separate hundreds against Northamptonshire. His centuries now number 40. Ames holds the wicket-keeping record with 127 wickets (c. 79, st. 48) in 1929. He dismissed 121 batsmen in 1928, 97 in 1930, and 100 in 1932.
ISSUED BY
JOHN PLAYER & SONS
BRANCH OF THE IMPERIAL TOBACCO CO.
(OF GREAT BRITAIN & IRELAND), LTD.

1937 Kent score 219 for the loss of two wickets in just 71 minutes, v Gloucestershire at Dover.

1948 Harold Gimblett hits 310 for Somerset v Sussex at Eastbourne, setting a new individual record for the county.

1965 Clive Inman (Leicestershire) scores the fastest first-class 50 v Nottinghamshire at Trent Bridge. The Notts bowlers, seeking a declaration, feed him full-tosses and he reaches his half-century in eight minutes off 13 balls.

AUGUST

21

1878 Surrey wicket-keeper Edward Pooley completes ten dismissals v Kent at The Oval, his tally including a world-record eight stumpings.

1914 Birth of Doug Wright at Sidcup, Kent. D.V.P.W. holds the world record of seven hat-tricks and in his first-class spinning career takes 2056 wickets at 23.98.

1986 Ian Botham goes to a world-record 356 Test dismissals v New Zealand at The Oval.

1988 Yorkshire beat Surrey by 3 wickets to win the inaugural women's County Championship final at Chingford.

Doug Wright, the hat-trick specialist.

22

1845 The Surrey Club is formed at The Horns, Kennington and the following year begin playing matches at The Oval. They win the official County Championship outright 15 times, including a record seven in succession in 1952–58.

1896 The Australians dismiss Gloucestershire for 17 at Cheltenham, the county's lowest first-class score.

1896 K.S. Ranjitsinhji (Sussex) sets a unique record of scoring two first-class centuries on the same day, v Yorkshire at Hove.

1934 Frank Woolley deputises for the injured Les Ames behind the stumps for England v Australia at The Oval and becomes, at 47 years 87 days, the oldest man to keep wicket in a Test match. He concedes a Test record 37 byes.

23

1909 Birth of Syd Buller at Leeds. One of the game's greatest umpires, he first keeps wicket for Yorkshire and Worcestershire and takes 249 first-class dismissals, then stands in 33 Test matches between 1956 and 1969.

1911 Fred Huish (Kent) sets a world record when he stumps nine Surrey batsmen in the match at The Oval.

1938 England declare at 903–7 v Australia at The Oval, the highest innings in Test cricket. Len Hutton's then world-record 364 is the second longest Test innings (797 minutes) after Hanif Mohammad (970 minutes).

1966 Bob Taylor (Derbyshire) dismisses seven Glamorgan batsmen in one innings at Derby, the first of the three occasions he performs the feat.

1851   Birth of Thomas Kendall at Bedford, England. He plays for Australia in the first-ever Test match v England in 1877 and his 7-55 in the second innings prepares the way for his adopted country's victory.

1938   Arthur Wellard (Somerset) equals the world record when he hits Frank Woolley (Kent) for five sixes in an over at Wells.

1972   Dennis Amiss scores the first century in a one-day international, v Australia at Old Trafford.

25

1928   Birth of Ken Suttle at Brook Green, London. The Sussex opener holds the record for making 423 consecutive County Championship appearances between 1954 and 1969, and scores 30,225 first-class runs at 31.09.

1968   Prolific Australian Test batsman Stan McCabe dies following a fall near his Sydney home. His most famous innings, still much talked-about and analysed: his run-a-minute 232* v England at Trent Bridge in 1938.

1973   A bomb scare halts play at Lord's for 89 minutes in the England v West Indies Test.

1986   Ian Botham equals the Test record of Andy Roberts and Sandeep Patil by scoring 24 runs in an over off Derek Stirling (New Zealand) at The Oval.

Len Hutton batting at The Oval in 1938.

AUGUST

26

1909   Middlesex beat Gloucestershire by an innings and 31 runs in a single day's play at Bristol. The star for Middlesex is Francis Tarrant who takes 13–67 and carries his bat through the Middlesex innings of 145.

1920   Percy Fender scores a century in 35 minutes for Surrey v Northants at Northampton. This remains the fastest century until equalled by Steve O'Shaughnessy (Lancashire) in 1983.

1924   Charlie Parker (Gloucestershire) completes his second hat-trick of the match v Middlesex at Bristol, and becomes the fourth of only seven men to achieve this remarkable feat.

1975   Robin Hobbs (Essex) scores a century in 44 minutes for Essex v Australians at Chelmsford, the fastest 100 for 55 years and the fourth fastest ever.

27

1908   Birth of Don Bradman at Cootamundra, New South Wales. His records are legend: 117 first-class centuries, 12 Test double centuries, and 6996 Test runs at 99.94.

1969   Mike Procter (Gloucestershire) hits six sixes off successive balls though not all from the same over. Batting against Somerset at Taunton he hits two off the last two balls of a Dennis Breakwell over, then after a maiden at the other end, hits four more in Breakwell's next over.

1973   Gary Sobers (West Indies) holds six catches in the Lord's Test v England, equalling the world record for an outfielder in Test cricket.

A proud signature on a memorable scorecard.

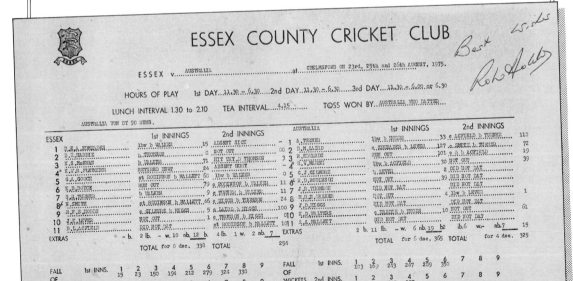

28

1914 Alonzo Drake (Yorkshire) bowls unchanged throughout both innings v Somerset at Weston-super-Mare. In the second innings he dismisses all ten batsmen in 42 balls.

1929 Frank Woolley (Kent) scores his 100th first-class century with 176 v Middlesex at Lord's, becoming the sixth player to reach that milestone.

1936 Arthur Wellard (Somerset) scores 30 runs in one over from T.R. Armstrong (Derbyshire) at Wells, hitting the last five balls for six.

1956 England retain the Ashes and Jim Laker ends the series with 46 wickets, second only to Sydney Barnes's world record of 49.

29

1882 England suffer one of their worst collapses in Test cricket. Needing only 85 runs in their second innings to win the Oval Test, they reach 51 for 2, then W.G. Grace is dismissed and the last six wickets fall for 11 runs; England lose by seven runs.

1906 George Hirst (Yorkshire) completes one of the best displays of all-round cricket v Somerset at Bath. He scores 111 and 117* and takes 6 for 70 and 5 for 45.

1977 Malcolm Nash, the bowler when Gary Sobers hit 36 runs in an over, is savaged by Frank Hayes (Lancashire) who hits 34 runs (6–4–6–6–6–6) and races to the second 50 of his 119 in 20 minutes.

1985 Graham Gooch and David Gower complete a Test partnership of 351 v Australia at The Oval.

30

1926 Jack Hobbs completes his highest individual score – 316* for Surrey v Middlesex at Lord's; it is the highest individual innings made at Lord's.

1949 Roly Jenkins (Worcestershire) performs his second hat-trick of the match v Surrey at Worcester, the last man to do so in England.

1979 Ian Botham completes the Test 'double' of 1000 runs and 100 wickets in his 21st Test, the lowest number of matches by any player.

31

1769 The first stroke-by-stroke account of a cricket match is recorded when the Duke of Dorset's XI play Wrotham. The scorecard includes the first known century, 107 by John Minshull.

1944 Birth of Clive Lloyd at Georgetown, Guyana, then British Guinea. He captains West Indies for a record 74 times in his 110 Test matches, scoring 7515 runs at 46.67.

1968 Gary Sobers (Nottinghamshire) hits Malcolm Nash (Glamorgan) for six sixes in one over, becoming the first man to score 36 runs in a first-class over.

1981 Ian Botham takes his 200th Test wicket v Australia at The Oval, the youngest man to do so and in the shortest time and in the fewest number of balls (9672).

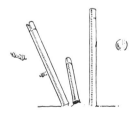

SEPTEMBER

1

1939   In what turns out to be his last county match Hedley Verity takes 7–9 for Yorkshire v Sussex at Hove. In the war he loses his life on active service.

1973   Gloucestershire win their first major honour since the 1877 Championship, beating Sussex by 40 runs at Lord's to win the Gillette Cup.

1984   Middlesex beat Kent in a dramatic finish to the NatWest final. With seven runs to get in the last over, they win off the last ball of the match.

1986   Ken Rutherford (New Zealand) scores 317 in a day v D.B. Close's XI at Scarborough. In an innings of 230 minutes, he hits eight sixes and 45 fours off 245 balls.

2

1878   Surrey bowler Edward Barrett, representing the Players XI, takes all ten Australian wickets for 43 runs at The Oval.

1972   Lancashire win the Gillette Cup for the third successive season, beating Warwickshire in the final by four wickets.

1978   An unlucky day in the Somerset year. For the second time Somerset reach a Gillette Cup final due to be played on 2 September, and again they lose – to Sussex by five wickets.

3

1882   Birth of John William Henry Tyler Douglas at Clapton. Often rising above his nickname 'Johnny Won't Hit Today', the Essex and England all-rounder and Test captain totals 24,531 first-class runs at 27.90 and 1893 wickets

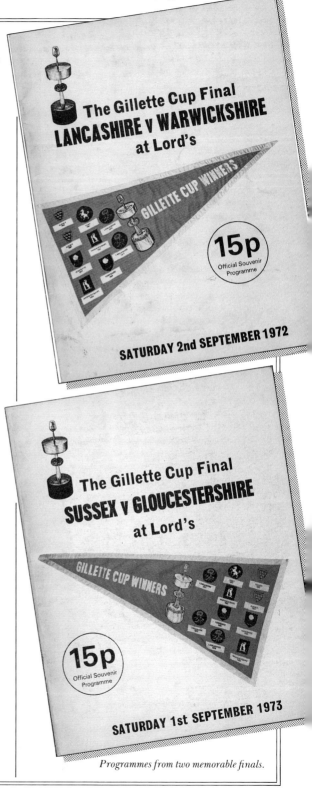

The Gillette Cup Final
LANCASHIRE v WARWICKSHIRE
at Lord's

GILLETTE CUP WINNERS

15p
Official Souvenir Programme

SATURDAY 2nd SEPTEMBER 1972

The Gillette Cup Final
SUSSEX v GLOUCESTERSHIRE
at Lord's

GILLETTE CUP WINNERS

15p
Official Souvenir Programme

SATURDAY 1st SEPTEMBER 1973

Programmes from two memorable finals.

J.W.H.T.DOUGLAS.

at 23.32. In 1908 he wins an Olympic gold medal as Britain's middleweight boxer.

1907   Gilbert 'The Croucher' Jessop scores 191 runs in 90 minutes for Gentlemen of the South v Players of the South at Hastings.

1983   Somerset avenge their 1967 defeat by Kent and win the NatWest final at Lord's by 24 runs. Vic Marks is man of the match.

4

1925   Jack Hobbs scores 266* for Players v Gentlemen at Scarborough, the highest individual innings in this fixture.

1947   Playing for South of England v South Africa at Hastings, Denis Compton completes his 17th century of the season, surpassing Jack Hobbs's 22-year-old record.

1965   Yorkshire (G. Boycott 146) record the biggest win in a Gillette Cup final, beating Surrey by 175 runs.

1976   Lancashire make their sixth and last appearance in a Gillette Cup final in the 1970s, losing to Northants by four wickets. In this remarkable sequence they win the trophy four times.

5

1909   Birth of Archie Jackson at Rutherglen, Scotland. After emigrating to Australia as a youngster he learns his senior-grade cricket in his new homeland and plays eight times for Australia, making 164 on his Test début. Sadly he dies at the age of 23.

1973   England and West Indies meet for the first time in a one-day international. In the Prudential Trophy match at Headingley the West Indies are bowled out for 181 and England hang on to win by one wicket (M. Denness 66).

1976   Five counties are capable of winning the John Player League on the last afternoon of the season. Somerset, the League leaders, lose the most exciting match in the League's history: pursuing Glamorgan's 191 for 7, they finish on 190 for 9. Kent take the title.

6

1880   The Oval plays host to the first Test match in England. W.G. Grace scores the first Test century on the ground and the home country beat Australia by five wickets.

1969   Yorkshire beat neighbours Derbyshire by 69 runs to win the Gillette Cup for the second time (1965 was their other year).

1980   Middlesex comfortably beat Kent by seven wickets to win the last Gillette Cup final. New sponsors NatWest take over the following year.

SEPTEMBER

SEPTEMBER

7

1859   George Parr's first English team to tour set sail from Liverpool, bound for North America and Canada. In the side are John Wisden, John Lillywhite, John 'Foghorn' Jackson who blew his nose after every wicket he took, Jemmy Grundy, Tom Hayward, A.J. 'Ducky' Diver, William Caffyn, Julius Caesar, H.H. Stephenson and Tom Lockyer.

1894   Birth of Victor York Richardson, grandfather of the Chappell brothers, in South Australia. Himself an Australian Test captain, he takes a record five catches in one innings v South Africa at Durban in 1935–36.

1963   In the first cup final to be played at Lord's, before a crowd of 25,000, Sussex beat Worcestershire by 14 runs to win the inaugural Gillette Cup.

George Parr and his party to tour the United States.

8

1880   The last day of the first Test match to be played in England. It is also the latest date on which Test cricket has been played in this country.

1966   Death of Edward Aspey English at Tiverton, Devon. The longest-lived first-class cricketer, he plays 18 matches for Hampshire in 1898–1901 and dies at the age of 102 years 250 days.

1979   After 104 years of trying, Somerset win their first major trophy, beating Northants by 45 runs to win the Gillette Cup final (Garner 6–29).

9

1853   Birth of Frederick Robert Spofforth at Balmain, New South Wales. Affectionately known as 'The Demon', he claims 853 first-class wickets at 14.95.

SEPTEMBER

Ted Dexter is the first captain to be presented with the Gillette Cup in 1963.

1894   Birth of Bert Oldfield at Sydney. His 90 dismissals v England is a record for an Australian 'keeper in the Ashes series.

1959   Death of West Indian all-rounder Collie Smith following injuries suffered in a car crash. His body is later flown back to Jamaica where some 60,000 attend his funeral. In his 26 Tests he scores 1331 runs at 31.69 and takes 48 wickets at 33.85.

10

1872   Birth of K.S. Ranjitsinhji in India. After winning his cricket Blue at Cambridge, 'Ranji' goes on to play for Sussex and England, scoring 154* on his Test début. He scores 24,692 first-class runs at 56.37 and takes 133 wickets at 34.59.

1948   Playing for East v West at Kingston, Middlesex bowler J.M. Sims takes 10–90 in 18.4 overs.

1978   Wicket-keeper Taslim Arif claims a Pakistani record with 10 dismissals in a match; he is playing for National Bank v Punjab at Lahore.

1986   Geoff Boycott begins his last first-class match for Yorkshire, v Northants.

11

1871   Launch of Scarborough Festival, albeit modestly, when a local team takes on a holidaymakers XI at Castle Hill.

1911   Birth of Lala Amarnath at Lahore. He scores a century on his Test début for India and goes on to captain his country. He shares with Walter Hadlee the distinction of being the father of two sons who both play Test cricket.

1985   Sri Lanka beat India by 149 runs at Colombo to register their first Test win. The next day is proclaimed a national holiday.

SEPTEMBER

1901   Playing for the Rest of England v Yorkshire at Lord's, C.B. Fry (105) scores his sixth successive first-class century, a world record since equalled by Don Bradman and Mike Procter.

1925   Jack Hobbs scores his 16th century of the season, playing for an English XI v Yorkshire, setting a record which survives until 1947 when Denis Compton goes two hundreds better.

1937   Birth of Wes Hall at Bridgetown. One of the game's greatest fast bowlers, he takes 192 Test wickets at 26.38.

mainstay of the county side in the late Twenties and Thirties, scoring 18,034 runs for the county at 37.64.

1977   Death of Arthur Fagg at Tunbridge Wells at the age of 62. The Kent and England opener holds the unique record of scoring two double centuries in the same match.

1983   Faced by the easy bowling of Leicestershire batsmen David Gower and James Whitaker, Steve O'Shaughnessy (Lancashire) equals Percy Fender's record for the fastest century, made in 35 minutes.

1902   Birth of Arthur Mitchell in Yorkshire. A dour opener, he becomes a

A day of many cricketing birthdays: Lancashire and England bowler Paul Allott **(1956)**; South African batsman

Arthur Mitchell (seated, extreme right) with other Yorkshire stalwarts of the 1930s.

Kepler Wessels, who later plays for Australia (**1957**); and New Zealanders Jeff Crowe (**1958**) and Brendon Bracewell (**1959**).

1928 On dismissing R.K. Tyldesley (Lancashire) in the final match of the season, Kent bowler 'Titch' Freeman, playing for Rest of England becomes the first and only man to take 300 wickets in a season, going on to a now unbeatable total of 304.

Micky Stewart – a troubled time as England's first team manager.

15

1946 Birth of Mike Procter at Durban, South Africa. One of the game's greatest all-rounders, he scores 21,934 first-class runs at 36.01, takes 1414 wickets at 19.48 and holds 325 catches.

1947 Denis Compton completes his record-breaking 18th century of the season, on his way to 246 for Middlesex v The Rest at The Oval.

1955 Birth of Abdul Qadir at Lahore. The Pakistani spinner and googly expert has a relatively high Test average but he continues to be one of those rare bowlers capable of turning a match at the highest level.

16

1899 In a minor match at Cane Hill, Surrey, 20-year-old Vivian Crawford scores a century in 19 minutes.

1932 Birth of Micky Stewart. The first England cricket manager, a Surrey and England player and distinguished amateur footballer, enters the world only five miles from his beloved Oval ground.

1961 Death of Percy (A.P.F.) Chapman at the age of 61. He scores 16,309 first-class runs at 31.97 and is remembered as

the first England captain to declare an innings in Australia, closing the second innings of the 1928–29 Brisbane Test at 342–8.

17

1940 Birth of Peter Lever at Todmorden, a disputed territory in Lancashire-Yorkshire. Opting for Lancashire he becomes a fine opening bowler and hero of many one-day triumphs, ending his first-class career with 796 first-class wickets at 25.59.

1982 Duleep Mendis, captain of Sri Lanka, scores the first of two hundreds in the inaugural Test v India.

1988 On the final day of the season Franklyn Stephenson (Notts) completes the double, with two centuries and 10 wickets in the match, the first man to achieve the feat since Richard Hadlee in 1984. They are the only two players to do so since the number of county championship matches was reduced in 1969.

SEPTEMBER

18

1937   Birth of Alphonso ('Alfie') Roberts in St Vincent. The first cricketer born outside the 'Big Five' islands to reach the West Indies Test team, he makes his début v New Zealand at Auckland in 1955–56 at the age of 18, scores 28 and 0 and is not selected again.

1958   Birth of Derek Pringle in Nairobi, Kenya. The Essex and England all-rounder shares a family record with the Amarnaths, Hadlees, etc. It is not so well known perhaps, but his father played for East Africa in the 1975 World Cup.

1958   Winston Davis is born in Kingstown, St Vincent. He makes his Test début against India at St Johns, Antigua in 1983 and goes on to play county cricket for Northamptonshire.

19

1919   Gil Langley is born in Adelaide. He becomes one of the safest of Australian wicket-keepers and averages almost four dismissals per match through his 26 Tests, enjoying four stumpings and three catches on his début against the West Indies at Brisbane in 1951.

1953   Wayne Clark is born in Perth, Western Australia. He is called into the Australian Test team when 12 regulars defect to World Series cricket and takes 44 wickets in his 10 Tests between December 1977 and March 1979.

1970   Death of G.T.S. Stevens, Middlesex and England leg-break bowler who took 684 first-class wickets at 26.84 and averaged 29.36 with the bat (10,376 runs).

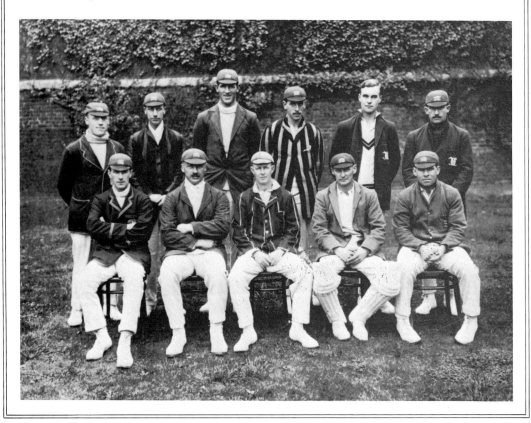

1982 F.T. Badcock dies in Perth, Western Australia. Born in India, Badcock is educated at Wellington College, Berks before going to live in New Zealand where he is selected to play in New Zealand's first Test match in 1930. He bags a 'pair' but goes on to make six more appearances.

20

1861 Birth in Adelaide of Walter Giffen, younger brother of the legendary George Giffen. He plays in 3 Tests but his career falters when he loses the top of two fingers in an accident in an Adelaide gasworks.

1893 Birth of F.W. Gilligan, Oxford University and Essex wicket-keeper.

1951 Birth of Stephen Boock at Dunedin. The left-arm spinner becomes New Zealand's most effective slow bowler of recent years.

21

1902 Birth of Learie Constantine in Trinidad. A great ambassador for the game, he is knighted for his services to cricket. A fast bowler and attacking bat, he becomes a great favourite on West Indies tours between 1923 and 1939 and in his seasons with Nelson in the Lancashire League.

1959 Birth of Richard Ellison at Ashford. The Kent medium-fast bowler makes his Test début in 1984 and is one of the five *Wisden* Cricketers of the Year in 1986.

G.T.S. Stevens (back row, second from right) in Pelham Warner's Championship-winning Middlesex team of 1920.

1982 Duleep Mendis becomes the first batsman to make the same three-figure score in each innings of a Test match in Sri Lanka's first official Test against India at Madras.

22

1859 The first England tourists arrive in Quebec for their tour of Canada and the United States.

1880 Death of G.F. Grace from pneumonia at Basingstoke, aged 29. The youngest of the three Test-playing Grace brothers, he had played only two weeks earlier in the first Test match on English soil.

1962 Birth of Martin Crowe at Auckland, New Zealand. One of the most stylish batsmen of his day.

1986 End of the second tied Test match, India v Australia at Madras. Maninder Singh is lbw to Greg Matthews.

23

1855 Birth of Sydney Pardon. Editor of *Wisden* from 1891 to 1925, he is the longest-serving editor of cricket's most respected book.

1952 Birth of Anshuman Gaekwad at Bombay. The son of India's captain on the 1959 tour of England, he scores two Test hundreds and is responsible for the slowest double century in first-class cricket, made in 652 minutes (426 balls) v Pakistan at Jullundur in 1983–84.

1979 After being no-balled 11 times in six overs, Rodney Hogg, the Australian fast bowler, bowls a beamer, tears up a stump, throws it on the ground and storms off the field as India accumulate 457–4 at Bangalore.

SEPTEMBER

A.G. Steel.

24

1858 Birth of Allan (A.G.) Steel in Liverpool. A fine amateur all-rounder, he captains England in 1886 and 1888 and becomes President of the MCC in 1902.

1859 England's pioneer tourists win their first match, defeating XXII of Lower Canada by eight wickets at Montreal.

1950 Birth of Mohinder Amarnath at Patiala. In 1986 he hits a hundred before lunch for Indians v Northants.

25

1771 The Hambledon Club, then cricket's lawmakers, respond to the challenge of Thomas 'Shock' White of Reigate, who one day appeared on the field with a bat as wide as the wicket. From now on the width of the bat is limited to 4¼ inches.

1946 Birth of Bishen Bedi at Amritsar, India. In the 1960s and '70s he is one of the world's outstanding slow bowlers, taking 266 Test wickets at 28.71.

1961 Student riots in Ahmadabad force the transfer of the Test match between India and New Zealand to the comparative calm of Bombay.

26

A notable birthday for cricketers from England, India, South Africa and Australia.

1876 Charles Benett Llewellyn, in Pietermaritzburg. After playing 15 times for South Africa, he arrives in England and plays for Hampshire between 1899 and 1910, later moving into League cricket. His first-class record for Hampshire reveals steady all-round ability: 8772 runs at 27.58 and 711 wickets at 24.66.

1931 Vijay Manjrekar, in Bombay. A steady scorer on the post-war international scene, he plays in 55 Tests for India and scores 3208 runs at 39.12.

1935 Bob (R.W.) Barber, in Manchester. An all-rounder with Lancashire, Warwickshire and England, he scores 6760 runs and takes 152 wickets in his nine seasons at Old Trafford (1954–62) then hits 5978 runs for Warwickshire and takes 197 wickets in the next seven seasons (1963–69).

1943 Ian Chappell, in Adelaide. The oldest of the three Test-playing Chappell brothers, and a successful if controversial Australian captain, he plays in 75 Test matches scoring 5345 runs at 42.42.

27

1934 Birth of Duncan Fletcher who is to become known for his role as captain and for his own personal contribution (69* and 6–42) in Zimbabwe's memorable victory over Australia at Trent Bridge in their Group match in the 1983 World Cup.

1957 Birth of Bill Athey at Middlesborough. After seven years in the Yorkshire side the right-handed batsman moves to Gloucestershire and succeeds to the captaincy for 1989.

1982 Eddie Hemmings becomes the last Englishman to take all ten wickets in an innings when he performs the feat for a touring International XI v West Indies XI at Kingston. His analysis is particularly interesting – 10–175 – the highest number of runs conceded by any bowler taking all ten wickets, and yet less than half the West Indian total of 419 which is the largest innings score to include the all-ten feat.

28

1906 Foundation of present Lincolnshire CCC, stalwarts of the Minor Counties competition.

1946 Birth of Majid Khan at Jullundur. A brilliant right-handed strokemaker with Cambridge University, Glamorgan and Pakistan, for whom he makes his début at the age of 18, his career is studded with feats of audacious scoring: 147 in 89 minutes for Pakistanis v Glamorgan at Swansea in 1967, including 13 sixes; a century before lunch v New Zealand at Karachi in 1976–77; and a total of 27,444 first-class runs at 43.01.

29

1908 Foundation of present Cheshire CCC. Eighty years later the Minor Counties team achieve the historic feat of beating Northamptonshire in the NatWest competition.

1934 Birth of Lance Gibbs at Georgetown. The fluid West Indian off-spinner achieves high success in Test cricket, and on his retirement his 309 wickets is a world record.

1941 Birth of David Steele at Stoke-on-Trent. A *Wisden* Cricketer of the Year in 1975 after his heroic Test début v Australia, he moves from Northants to Derbyshire after 16 seasons then returns to Northants.

30

1869 One of the bravest or most foolhardy of cricketers is born in South Australia – Ernest Jones – the man whose reply to scoffing remarks by W.G. about his bowling ability is to send down a ball in the first match of the Australians' 1896 tour which passes through the Doctor's beard. He is also on record as the first man to be no-balled for throwing in a Test match.

1922 Birth of Allan Rae in Jamaica. Opening bat on the famous 1950 West Indies tour to England, he goes on to become a respected administrator in the golden era of West Indian cricket in the 1970s and '80s.

1969 India complete a 60-run win over New Zealand at Bombay after the match is switched at short notice from Ahmedabad, which is prevented from staging its first Test match by rioting in the city. Ahmedabad had to wait until November 1983 to become the 56th Test venue.

SEPTEMBER

OCTOBER

PLAYER'S CIGARETTES

T. W. GODDARD

THIS SURFACE IS ADHESIVE ASK YOUR TOBACCONIST FOR THE ATTRACTIVE ALBUM (PRICE ONE PENNY) SPECIALLY PREPARED TO HOLD THE COMPLETE SERIES

CRICKETERS 1938
A SERIES OF 50

10
T. W. GODDARD
(Gloucestershire and England)
Taking 248 wickets in 1937, average 16·76—more wickets than any other bowler that season in first-class cricket—Tom Goddard set the seal on a remarkable career. He first appeared for Gloucestershire as a fast bowler. He was allowed to leave, but showed so much promise on turning his attention to slow off-spin bowling while with the M.C.C. ground staff at Lord's, that Gloucestershire were recommended to re-engage him. In nine years Goddard has taken altogether 1,549 wickets. He played for England v. Australia in 1930, and against New Zealand in 1937, during which season he took all ten Worcestershire wickets at Cheltenham. Born October 1st, 1900.

JOHN PLAYER & SONS
BRANCH OF THE IMPERIAL TOBACCO CO.
(OF GREAT BRITAIN & IRELAND) LTD.

1

1900   Birth of Tom Goddard at Gloucester. After several seasons with the county as a fast bowler, he converts to off-breaks and begins a remarkable run of success with 184 wickets in the 1929 season. His best hauls are 248 wickets in 1937 and 238 in 1947, and his first-class total is 2979 at only 19.84 runs apiece.

1926   Birth of Roy Booth at Marsden, Yorkshire. The wicket-keeper plays first for his native county then moves to Worcestershire (1955–70). In 1964 he becomes the last 'keeper to take 100 dismissals in a season.

1937   Birth of the 'stormy petrel' of Pakistan cricket, Saeed Ahmed, at Jullundur. Half-brother to Younis Ahmed, he plays in 41 Tests scoring 2291 runs at 40.42. His Test career ends after a confrontation with Dennis Lillee; he drops out of the Test and is sent home for indiscipline.

2

1873   Birth of Pelham (P.F. or 'Plum') Warner in Trinidad. He captains the MCC tourists to Australia of 1903–04 and guides Middlesex from 1908 to 1920 when they win the County Championship. His runs for the county total 19,507 at 37.51. He becomes the founding editor of *The Cricketer* magazine and is knighted for his services to the game.

1933   Birth of A.W. Catt who is to become a loyal deputy to Godfrey Evans in the Kent side. When Alan Knott takes over the first team place in 1964 Catt moves to South Africa where he plays for Western Province. He is best remembered for the 48 byes conceded in one innings against Northampton in 1955 when he was suffering from the effects of the sun.

1964   The South Africans selected to tour Australia prove their worth in a match v Rest of South Africa at Johannesburg, scoring 618–4 on the first day (R.G. Pollock 123, A.J. Pithey 110, K.C. Bland 151*, D.T. Lindsay 107*).

3

1862   Birth of Johnny Briggs at Sutton-in-Ashfield, Notts. he learns the art of bowling relatively late but produces phenomenal figures for Lancashire and England, including 15–28 v South Africa at Cape Town in 1888–89. Prone to mental illness, he breaks down in a Test match and dies in the asylum at Cheadle aged 39.

1921   Birth of Ray Lindwall at Sydney. Australia's chief strike bowler in the post-war years, he takes 228 Test wickets at 23.03.

1964   The Nawab of Pataudi emulates his father by scoring a century in his first Test innings against Australia. He scores an undefeated 128 for India at Madras, while his father, playing for England on the 'bodyline' tour scored 102 at Perth.

4

1804   Birth of Nicholas Wanostracht at Camberwell. Known to cricketers as Felix, he is a fluent scorer for Kent in their great early years. He invents a bowling machine so menacing that no-one dares use it. Legend has it that the machine, the Catapulta, was more attractive to the British Army than to any cricketing body.

1926   Formation of the Women's Cricket Association

1962   Death of Patsy Hendren in South London, aged 73. He is second only to Jack Hobbs as a first-class century-maker, scoring 170 in his career.

Patsy Hendren of Middlesex, in England touring blazer.

5

1932   Birth of Madhav Apte at Bombay. He plays in only seven Tests for India but emerges with the remarkably high average of 49.27, including 163* v West Indies at Port of Spain. One of his opening partners is his brother, Arvind, who tours England in 1959 though is not selected for a Test match.

1940   Birth of Bob Cowper in Victoria. Following his international father, who plays Rugby for Australia, he makes his Test début in 1964. He later becomes a millionaire businessman with interests in Monte Carlo, organising several sports events in France, championing the cause of World Series Cricket and bidding for an Americas Cup challenge.

1983   Sandeep Patil is called up for India's 3rd Test against Pakistan when Mohinder Amarnath goes ill on the morning of the match. A special aircraft flies him 600 miles to Nagpur but he still misses the first day's play.

OCTOBER

1887 Birth of George Brown at Cowley, Oxford. An all-rounder who bowls and bats for Hampshire and bats and keeps wicket for England, in his first-class career he scores 22,959 runs for his county and takes 602 wickets; he is also credited with 530 dismissals including 53 stumpings.

1930 Birth of Richie Benaud at Penrith, New South Wales. The Australian all-rounder and captain achieves fame as an inspired leader, match-winning leg-break bowler and most imitated commentator since John Arlott's radio days.

Richie Benaud meets the Queen at Lord's in 1956.

1946 Birth of Tony Greig at Queenstown, South Africa. Qualifying for England, the competitive all-rounder becomes captain of the side and the first man to score a Test century and take five wickets in an innings in the same match. In his 58 Tests he scores 3599 runs at 40.43 and takes 141 wickets at 32.20.

1887 Birth of C.A.G. Russell in the East End of London. The Essex and England batsman is little remembered today but his 910 runs in Test cricket were achieved with an average of 56.87. He ends his Test career in 1922–23 with a century in each innings v South Africa at Durban (140 and 111), the first Englishman and the second player ever to achieve this feat.

Tony Greig in World Series Cricket colours and watched by team manager Gary Sobers.

1952 Birth of Graham Yallop in Victoria. He establishes himself in the Australian side after the defection of several members to World Series Cricket, becomes captain for a while and plays several notable innings including 268 v Pakistan at Melbourne in 1983–84.

1979 Geoff Dymock becomes the first Australian to dismiss all eleven opponents in the course of a Test match when he bowls Dilip Doshi to end India's second innings at Kanpur.

1928 Birth of Neil Harvey in Victoria. The left-handed bat with whom all others

of the post-war period have to stand comparison, he makes his first impact on the 1948 Australian tour of England when only 19. In Test cricket he scores 6149 runs at 48.41.

1945 Birth of Vanburn Holder in Barbados. A popular performer with Worcestershire and West Indies, he plays in 40 Tests and takes 582 wickets for his county at 23.11.

1986 Playing for South Australia v Tasmania at Adelaide, David Hookes (306*) and Wayne Phillips (213*) complete a record Australian partnership for all wickets when they add 462* in 299 minutes off 84.3 overs.

9

1951 Geoff Cook is born in Middlesbrough. As captain of Northamptonshire he scores a century in the first NatWest Trophy final in 1981, wins the Man of the Match award and a place on England's tour to India but finishes on the losing side.

1960 Railways of Pakistan beat Jammu and Kashmir by 10 wickets at Srinagar. After declaring at 236–0 they win by scoring 16–0 in their second innings and become only the third team to win a first-class match without losing a wicket (the other two are Lancashire and Karachi 'A').

1976 Notable performances by two opposing débutants at Lahore. Javed Miandad scores 163 in his first Test innings but is then dismissed by New Zealand off-spinner Peter Petherick who goes on to dismiss Wasim Raja and Intikhab Alam with his next two deliveries. This makes Petherick the second bowler (the other being M.J.C. Allom in 1930) to take a hat-trick on his Test début.

OCTOBER

1884 Birth of Neville Knox at Clapham, London. Thought the fastest bowler of his day in the mid-1900s, he takes 121 wickets for Surrey in 1905 and 129 in 1906, and before a skin disease ends his career in 1910 he captures 347 wickets for the county at 20.94.

1919 Birth of Gerry Gomez at Port-of-Spain, Trinidad. Veteran of 58 Tests, he becomes a steady-scoring bat and successful bowler, later a West Indian selector, stand-in Test umpire, administrator and radio commentator.

1956 Fazal Mahmood completes match figures of 13–114 on a matting wicket at Karachi as Pakistan move towards victory in their first Test match against Australia.

1964 A serious stomach disorder, developing after the start of play in the 2nd Test at Bombay, rules Norman O'Neill out of both innings and plays a part in allowing India to gain their second Test win against Australia – by two wickets.

1902 In the first Test between South Africa and Australia, H.M. Taberner captains the home country at Johannesburg in his only Test appearance. He scores 2 and returns bowling figures of 0–23 and 1–25.

1943 Birth of Keith Boyce in Barbados. A fierce competitor with Essex and West Indies, he takes 853 wickets and hits 8800 runs, usually at the rate of one per ball.

1956 First day of the first Test between Pakistan and Australia, at Karachi. Play is marked by extreme caution and produces an all-time record low output of runs in a Test match – 95 for the day. Australia

crawl to 80 in 53.1 overs, then the home side face Lindwall and Miller and manage 15–2 by close of play.

1861 Birth of Freddie Martin at Dartford. The Kent bowler goes on to enjoy a remarkable two-match Test career, taking 6–50 and 6–52 v Australia in 1890 and 2–39 in 24.3 overs v South Africa in 1892, giving him an international average of 10.07.

1911 Birth of Vijay Merchant at Bombay. His great scoring feats include 359* for Bombay v Maharashtra in 1944 and he ends his career with the remarkable first-class average of 72.74.

1925 Birth of Gilbert Parkhouse at Swansea. One of the few Welshmen to play cricket for England, he plays in seven Tests and opens the batting for Glamorgan for 18 years, scoring 22,619 runs at 31.81.

Vijay Merchant (right) opens the batting for India with Mushtaq Ali at The Oval in 1946.

13

1877 Birth of B.J.T. Bosanquet at Enfield. Beginning as a fast-medium bowler, he experiments with spin and develops the googly or 'Bosie', the off-break bowled with a leg-break action, and successfully introduces it on the county circuit for Middlesex in 1900. His career figures give him 268 wickets at 27.13 plus, for a specialist bowler, the enviable total of 6593 first-class runs at 35.26.

1941 Birth of John Augustine Snow at Peopleton, Worcestershire. The Sussex fast bowler and part-time poet is a notable successor to Fred Trueman in the England team and takes 202 Test wickets at 26.66.

1955 Pakistan win their first Test v New Zealand, at Karachi, by an innings and one run.

Rohan Kanhai, first choice wicket-keeper for the West Indies in 1957, and (right) in his more accustomed role as batsman at The Oval in 1982.

1982 Rohan Kanhai takes the field for an International XI in Pakistan and establishes a West Indian record of playing first-class cricket for 26 years 50 days.

OCTOBER

OCTOBER

14

1882   Birth of Charlie (C.W.L.) Parker near Gloucester. He lies third in the list of wicket-takers in first-class cricket, though his 3278 victims earn him scant reward from the England selectors who pick him only once, v Australia at Old Trafford in 1921.

1914   Birth of Tom Dollery at Reading. A great success as Warwickshire's first professional captain, leading them to the Championship in 1951, he too, like Parker, is largely overlooked by the selectors and plays only four times for England.

1982   Sunil Gavaskar completes a world Test record for any 12 months of the year with 1984 runs in 27 innings (2 not out) for an average of 79.36.

15

1864   Formation of the original Somerset CCC. The present club dates from 1875.

1935   Birth of Jimmy Binks at Hull. He makes his début as Yorkshire wicket-keeper in 1955 and, 412 consecutive games later, retires in 1969. In his two Tests, v India in 1963–64, he is elevated to opening batsman, and in the second match takes five catches in India's first innings.

16

1876   Birth of Jimmy Sinclair in South Africa. He scores his country's first Test century and plays for both South Africa and England at Rugby Union.

1952   Pakistan play their first Test match, v India at Delhi.

1987   Newspaper reports after the hurricane over England claim that 27 cricket pavilions were blown away and six of the oaks around the Sevenoaks ground were uprooted.

Martin Donnelly, a Lord's specialist.

17

1917   Birth of Martin Donnelly in North Island, New Zealand. Along with A.P.F. Chapman he holds the distinction of scoring a century in the Varsity match at Lord's, for Gentlemen v Players at the same ground and for New Zealand in a Lord's Test.

1952   In the first India v Pakistan Test the Indian last-wicket pair H.R. Adhikari (81*) and Ghulam Ahmed (50) put on a series record of 109.

1955   New Zealand take 108.3 overs to score 124 in their second innings v Pakistan at Karachi.

18

1902   J.H. Anderson captains South Africa in his only Test match, v Australia. He scores 32 and 11.

1983   Death of V.L. Manjrekar at Madras, aged 52. One of the finest batsmen to represent India, he played in 55 Tests scoring 3208 runs at 39.12.

1978   Death of Frank Woolley at Halifax, Nova Scotia, aged 91.

Harold Gimblett, a prolific scorer for Somerset throughout his career.

1914   Birth of Harold Gimblett at Bicknoller. In 20 years with Somerset he scores more than 21,000 runs but plays only three times for England. Against Sussex at Eastbourne in 1948 he hits 310; he scores 49 centuries for the county and tops 1000 runs in 12 seasons.

20

1917   Birth of Ken Cranston at Liverpool. He plays county cricket for only two seasons, 1947–48, going straight in as Lancashire's captain. He scores 1928 runs at 40.16 and takes 142 wickets at 23.00, and plays eight times for England. He gives it all up for dentistry.

1957   Karachi 'A' become the second team after Lancashire to win a first-class match without losing a wicket. After declaring at 277–0 they beat Sind 'A' by an innings and 77 runs.

1969   On the final day of the 3rd Test at Hyderabad, New Zealand are in sight of a series victory. India, needing 268 to win, slump to 76–7 before heavy rain drives the players from the field. Sunshine follows, but too late; the match is called off and the series drawn 0–0.

W. H. PONSFORD.
VICTORIA

CARRERAS
HIGH-CLASS CIGARETTES

W. H. PONSFORD
(Australia and Victoria)

Opening batsman who has also been a prolific run-getter, he held the world's record with a score of 437 for Victoria during season 1927-28, returning the terrific average of 152.12. Playing his initial Test innings against England in 1924-25, he joined the select band of batsmen who have scored a century in their first match.

A Series of Cricketers No. 16

ARCADIA WORKS
LONDON·ENGLAND

19

1900   Birth of Bill Ponsford in Victoria. In the 1930s he and Bradman are the world's most prolific batsmen. Ponsford twice scores more than 400, and finishes his career with a first-class average of 65.18.

OCTOBER

 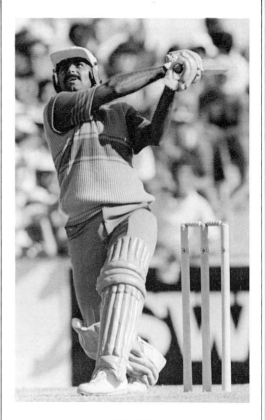

Qasim Omar (above) and Javed Miandad (above right) in Australia shortly after their successful partnership.

21

1931   Birth of Jim Parks at Haywards Heath. One of England's regular post-war wicket-keepers, appearing in 46 Tests, he scores more than 1000 runs for Sussex in 18 seasons and in 1959 claims 90 victims in the season (84 caught, 6 stumped).

1961   England win their first Test in Pakistan, at Lahore, by five wickets. Captain for the series is E.R. Dexter.

1985   Qasim Omar (206) and Javed Miandad (203*) add 397 for the 3rd wicket for Pakistan v Sri Lanka at Faisalabad. Omar is later 'banished' after revelations about drug-taking.

22

1883   Death of George Coulthard from consumption, aged 27. As England's touring umpire he provokes a riot with his controversial run-out decision at Sydney in the match v New South Wales. As a player he becomes a Test cricketer for Australia.

1961   Peter Richardson and Geoff Pullar open England's first innings in an official Test in Pakistan. The partnership generates just two runs.

1967   Ian Brayshaw becomes the third bowler in Sheffield Shield history to take all ten wickets. Playing for Western Australia v Victoria at Perth, he collects his haul in 17.6 overs for 44 runs; among his victims are Lawry, Redpath, Cowper and Stackpole.

become the first brothers to open a Test innings since W.G. and E.M. Grace in 1880.

1976   Sadiq Mohammad sets a record with another brother, Mushtaq. Sadiq (103) and Mushtaq (101) become the second brothers after the Chappells to score a century in the same innings, as Pakistan proceed to 473–8 dec v New Zealand at Hyderabad.

1982   Bob Taylor breaks John Murray's world record of 1527 victims during the England XI v Queensland match at Brisbane.

Bob Taylor, record-breaking wicket-keeper.

23

1900   Birth of Douglas Jardine at Bombay. One of England's most controversial captains, he is chiefly remembered for his leadership tactics on the Bodyline tour. In his 22 Tests he scores 1296 runs at 48.00.

1941   Birth of Colin Milburn at Burnopfield, Co. Durham. A skilful and luxuriously built hitter, he loses the sight of his left eye in a car crash at the age of 27. He regains his county place for a short while but is then compelled to retire.

1952   The Test between India and Pakistan at Lucknow is played on jute matting. Pakistan go on to win their second-ever Test match.

24

1966   Khalid Ibadulla scores 166 on the first day of the only Pakistan v India Test at Karachi. He bats all day and becomes the first Pakistani to score a century on his Test début.

1969   When the Mohammad brothers, Hanif and Sadiq, open the batting for Pakistan v New Zealand at Karachi, they

25

1952   Nazar Mohammad (124*) scores Pakistan's first Test century v India at Lucknow.

1975   Playing for United Bank v Multan at Karachi, Khalid Irtiza and Aslam Ali add a world record 456 runs for the 3rd wicket.

1978   Nineteen-year-old Amin Lakhani, playing for Pakistan Universities & Youth XI v Indians at Multan, completes his second hat-trick of the match. He becomes the seventh player to perform the feat in first-class cricket, and is the last to do so.

OCTOBER

Harry Lee (second from left), one of four century-makers for Middlesex against Sussex at Lord's in 1920.

26

1890   Birth of Harry (H.W.) Lee at Marylebone. A Middlesex regular of the inter-war years, opening bat Lee plays 666 innings for his county, scoring 18,594 runs at 29.94. Also a useful bowler, he claims 340 wickets for Middlesex at 32.54.

1952   Pakistan record their first Test win in only their second match. At Lucknow they defeat India by an innings and 43 runs. Fazal Mahmood takes 7–42 in India's second innings.

1969   Hanif Mohammad is dismissed for the last time in Test cricket. He has missed only two of Pakistan's first 57 matches.

27

1963   Playing for New South Wales v Queensland at Brisbane, Bobby Simpson completes his innings of 359, the highest post-war score by an Australian. A year later he is playing in a Test v Pakistan at Karachi and scores a century in each innings.

1977   Tasmania join the Sheffield Shield and become cricket's latest first-class state.

1983   Sunil Gavaskar (121) passes Geoffrey Boycott's world record of 8114 Test runs in the India v West Indies match at Delhi.

1986   West Indies are dismissed for 53 by Pakistan at Faisalabad (Imran Khan 4–30, Abdul Qadir 6–16), their lowest-ever Test score.

28

1877 Birth of G.J. Thompson at Cogenhoe near Northampton. Known as the 'Northampton Nugget', he becomes his county's first Test cricketer, playing six times for England. Although selected for his medium-fast bowling (1078 first-class wickets at 18.88) he also performs well with the bat, scoring more than 8000 runs for Northants.

1928 Birth of D.K. Gaekwad at Baroda. He becomes captain of the 1959 Indian tourists to England, guiding the fortunes of players such as Pankaj Roy, P.R. Umrigar and wicket-keeper P.G. Joshi.

1978 Bishen Bedi plays in his 60th Test to pass P.R. Umrigar as India's most capped player. He goes on to reach 67 but with the increase in the amount of Test cricket this total is passed by several players in the 1980s.

29

1861 Birth of C. Stewart Caine who is to become Editor of *Wisden* from 1926–1933.

1927 New South Wales score 571 in a day v New Zealanders at Sydney. J.M. Gregory (152) hits a century before lunch, and other players to score a hundred are T.J.E. Andrews (134), A.F. Kippax (119) and A. Jackson (104).

1984 Mudassar Nazar is pipped for a Test double century v India at Faisalabad. On 199, he is caught behind. This is the only innings of 199 in Test history.

30

1903 Birth of J.L. Hopwood who is to become one of the great stalwarts of Lancashire cricket between the wars. Between 1923 and 1939 he scores over 15,000 runs and takes more than 600 wickets for the county.

1955 Imtiaz Ahmed (209) becomes the first wicket-keeper to score a double century in a Test match (Pakistan v New Zealand at Lahore).

1976 Majid Khan (Pakistan) becomes the fourth player to score a century before lunch on the first day of a Test match, v New Zealand at Karachi.

31

1889 England's first tourists to India set sail from Tilbury Docks.

1976 In the Karachi Test v New Zealand, Javed Miandad continues Pakistan's domination with an innings of 206, becoming at 19 years 141 days the youngest man to score a Test match double century.

1982 Playing for Pakistan International Airways v Karachi, Zaheer Abbas scores two centuries in a first-class match for a record eighth time.

NOVEMBER

1

1865 Birth of Monty Bowden at Stockwell, London. The Surrey wicket-keeper becomes, at 23 years 144 days, England's youngest Test captain – v South Africa at Cape Town in 1888–89.

1919 Birth of S.A. Banerjee, the Indian fast bowler, who was to take 4 wickets in his first innings against the West Indies at Calcutta – the first with his 5th ball – but this was to be his only Test appearance.

1923 Birth of Bruce Dooland at Adelaide. The Australian all-rounder plays three times for his country before arriving in Britain where he plays League cricket and then joins Nottinghamshire. Between 1953 and 1957 he takes 100 wickets every season with his leg-breaks and googlies, and twice achieves the double.

1951 Craig Serjeant is born in Perth. He is to make his Test début at Lord's in 1977 where he top-scores for Australia in the Jubilee Test, celebrating 25 years of the reign of Queen Elizabeth II.

2

1877 Birth of Victor Trumper at Sydney. One of Australia's cricketing legends, he is regarded as that country's best batsman before Bradman and averages nearly 40, on poor pitches, in his 48 Tests.

1891 Birth of Harry Elliott at Scarcliffe, Derbyshire. He keeps wicket for his county for 27 years, and plays his last first-class match at the age of 55. He is capped once for England.

1935 Death of Jock (H.B.) Cameron at the age of 30, after catching fever on his return from South Africa's tour to England. A fine wicket-keeper batsman, he once hit Hedley Verity for 30 runs in an over.

3

1863 Foundation of the first Gloucestershire CCC. The present club dates from 1871.

1899 Foundation of the present Derbyshire CCC at the Guildhall, Derby.

1928 On making exactly 100 for MCC at Victoria at Melbourne, Patsy Hendren becomes the fifth man to reach the milestone of 100 first-class centuries.

Victor Trumper.

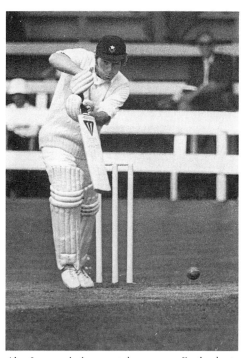

Alan Jones, unlucky never to have won an England cap.

1938   Birth of Alan Jones at Swansea. The heaviest-scoring batsman in Glamorgan's history, he amasses 36,049 first-class runs at 32.89, more than anyone else not awarded a Test cap.

1947   Birth of Rodney Marsh at Armdale, Perth. His 355 Test dismissals are a world record for a wicket-keeper; in his 94 Tests he also compiles 3558 runs at 26.75.

1979   Syed Kirmani becomes only the third recognised 'night-watchman' to score a century in Test cricket. After being promoted to No. 5, he goes on to make 101* before India declare against Australia at Bombay.

1901   Birth of Eddie Paynter at Oswaldtwistle. The Lancashire and England left-hander combines pugnacious defence with sharp attacking play and is remembered both for scoring 83 in nearly four hours in a Test at Brisbane, and for hitting 322 runs in a day v Sussex at Hove. In 20 Tests he scores 1540 at the fine average of 59.23.

1921   First day of a three-Test series between South Africa and Australia, in Durban, arranged to break the Australians' boat journey on the way home from England.

1964   Death of Peter, the Lord's cat. He is the only animal to receive an obituary in *Wisden*.

Rodney Marsh in jubilant mood as he catches Allan Lamb at Perth in 1982.

NOVEMBER

6

1897 Birth of Jack O'Connor at Cambridge. He becomes an Essex regular between 1921 and 1939, hitting a record 71 centuries for the county and spinning his way to 537 wickets.

1952 Birth of B.J. McKechnie in New Zealand. He represents his country at both Rugby Union and cricket, scores a penalty v Wales in 1978 and is the unfortunate recipient of Trevor Chappell's notorious underarm ball.

1956 Birth of Graeme Wood at Fremantle. The Australian opener becomes a Test regular after the Packer Affair, and in 1980 scores 112 in the Centenary Test at Lord's.

7

1876 Birth of Ted Arnold at Exmouth. He achieves the 'double' four years in succession from 1899, helping Worcestershire to consolidate after achieving first-class status. In the 1903–04 Ashes series he dismisses Victor Trumper with his first ball in Test cricket and finishes second in the series bowling averages behind Wilfred Rhodes.

1914 Playing for Queensland v New South Wales at Brisbane, James Sheppard becomes the first outfielder in Australia to hold six catches in an innings.

1977 Karnataka beat Kerala by an innings and 186 runs, the fourth team to win a first-class match without losing a wicket. After dismissing their opponents for 141 they make 451–0 dec and bowl out Kerala a second time for 124.

8

1917 Death in action in Belgium of Colin Blythe, aged 38. The Kent and England slow left-arm bowler enjoyed remarkable success between 1899 and 1914, taking 2210 first-class wickets for his county at 16.68. A statue at the Canterbury ground commemorates his loss.

1959 Worsening international relations bring the cancellation of a tour to South Africa by a side captained by Frank Worrell. The planned itinerary includes matches against black teams.

1987 In the World Cup final at Eden Gardens, Calcutta, Australia score 253–5 to defeat England by seven runs (246–8).

9

1943 Birth of John Shepherd in Barbados. On the county circuit he gives excellent service to Kent and Gloucestershire, finding a special place in the limited-overs game. A valued cricketing ambassador, he is the first black man to play in South Africa's Currie Cup.

1985 Richard Hadlee (New Zealand) dismisses nine Australian batsmen for 52 at Brisbane, the fourth best return in Test cricket.

1986 Pakistan are dismissed by West Indies at Lahore for 77, their lowest home total (Courtney Walsh 4–21, Tony Gray 3–20).

10

1933 Birth of Seymour Nurse in Barbados. His Test batting figures of 2523 runs at 47.60 testify to his excellence. In his final Test, v New Zealand at Christchurch in 1958–59, he scores 258.

1948 The Feroz Shah Kotla stadium in Delhi stages its first Test, between India and West Indies. More than 1300 runs are scored in the five days, and although the result is a draw the crowd is memorably entertained, in particular by Clyde Walcott (152) and Everton Weekes (128).

1972 Death of Charlie Hallows at Bolton, aged 77. In May 1928 the Lancashire and England bat scores 1000 runs, a feat then achieved only by W.G. Grace and W.R. Hammond.

11

1891 George Giffen (South Australia) completes the most remarkable all-round performance in first-class cricket. Against Victoria at Adelaide he scores 271 and then takes 9–96 and 7–70 to bring his side victory by an innings and 164 runs.

1969 New Zealand win their first Test series after a drawn match at Dacca. Pakistan, set 184 to win in 2 hours, reach 51–4 when a riot breaks out but it fails to save them.

1977 Victoria opener Paul Hibbert scores 100 v Indian tourists without hitting a boundary, the only time this act of omission has been achieved in Australia.

1983 Wayne Phillips scores 159 on his Test début for Australia v Pakistan at Perth. His stand of 259 with Graham Yallop sets an all-wicket record for Australia-Pakistan matches.

Richard Hadlee, the most successful Test match bowler of the 1980s.

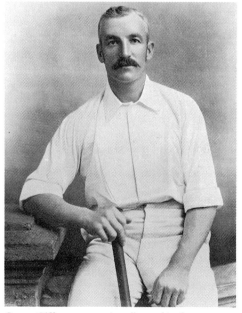

George Giffen – an amazing all-round performance.

NOVEMBER

12

1921 Jack Gregory scores the fastest century in Test cricket. Playing for Australia v South Africa at Johannesburg, he speeds to his hundred in 70 minutes.

1983 Ahmadabad becomes the latest venue for Test cricket. Completed in seven months, the stadium holds 60,000 spectators. In the West Indies' second innings Kapil Dev takes 9–83, and Clive Lloyd's reaction is to suggest that more care should have been taken with the wicket!

1985 New Zealand win a Test in Australia for the first time, at Brisbane by an innings and 41 runs (Richard Hadlee 15–123, Martin Crowe 188).

13

1858 Birth of P.S. McDonnell at Kensington, London. As a child he goes to Australia, and as a man returns four times to England with Australian touring teams. The attacking right-hander scores 147 v England at Sydney in 1881–82 and captains the 1888 touring side.

1940 Birth of Jack Birkenshaw at Rothwell, Yorkshire. He plays first for Yorkshire, then for Leicestershire where he spent 20 seasons, scoring 11,040 runs at 23.79 and taking 908 wickets at 26.49.

1982 Norman Cowans (Middlesex) becomes England's 500th Test cricketer.

14

1904 Birth of Harold Larwood at Nuncargate, Notts. England's most famous inter-war strike bowler makes his Test début at 21 and is a key figure on the Bodyline tour of 1932–33, taking 33

wickets at 19.51. The constant effort on hard grounds damages a toe joint and effectively ends his Test career. In 1950 he emigrates to Australia.

1967 Death of C.K. Nayudu at Indore at the age of 72. India's first Test captain, he once hit 11 sixes in an innings for Hindus v MCC at Bombay in 1926–27.

Monument to C.K. Nayudu at Indore.

1983 Carl Rackemann completes match figures of 11–118 against Pakistan to record the best Test figures at Perth. This is the first Test in Australia in which wides and no-balls are scored against the bowler's analysis.

1983 Indian substitute fielder Gursharan Singh takes three catches against the West Indies while deputising for the injured Roger Binny at Ahmedabad. Having already taken a catch in the first innings he becomes the first substitute to take four catches in a Test match.

NOVEMBER

15

1869   Birth of F.H. Huish at Clapham. As Kent wicket-keeper between 1895 and 1914 he sets a record of 1328 dismissals.

1903   Birth of C.S. Dempster at Wellington, New Zealand. The first man to score a Test century for his country, he later plays country house cricket for Sir Julien Cahn's XI and joins Leicestershire. In his five seasons for the county he hits 4659 runs at 49.04.

1947   Don Bradman hits his 100th first-class century, for an Australian XI v Indians at Sydney.

1959   Death of Alex Kennedy at Southampton, aged 68. In his Hampshire career he takes 2549 wickets at 21.16, and 31 Test wickets at 19.32.

16

1862   Birth of Charlie (C.T.B.) Turner at Bathurst, New South Wales. He takes 993 first-class wickets at 14.24 and 101 Test wickets at 16.53. On his first tour of England he takes 314 wickets and two years later returns and takes 215 more. Not surprisingly, he is nicknamed 'The Terror'.

1940   Birth of Chris Balderstone at Huddersfield. He makes his début for Yorkshire in 1961 and moves to Leicestershire in 1971; he receives his first England cap in 1976. The right-handed bat is also a keen soccer player and has spells at Huddersfield Town, Carlisle United and Doncaster Rovers. On one occasion he plays county cricket and League football on the same day.

1956   Opening of The Wanderers ground at Johannesburg, to replace the Old Wanderers, which became a marshalling yard, and the Ellis Park Rugby ground.

17

1923   Birth of Bert Sutcliffe at Auckland. One of New Zealand's greatest batsmen, his 385 for Otago v Canterbury at Christchurch in 1952–53 is the eighth highest first-class innings of all time and the highest made in New Zealand. In first-class cricket he amasses 17,283 runs at 47.22.

1959   A dull day in Dacca. Pakistan creep unwillingly from 73–4 to 134 and Australia, set 110 to win, manage 64–1 by close of play. Richie Benaud (39.3–26–42–4) and Slasher Mackay (45–27–42–6) are mainly responsible for paralysing the Pakistani batsmen.

1975   Rodney Marsh equals Arnold Long's record of 11 catches in a first-class match. He performs the feat playing for Western Australia v Victoria at Perth.

Turner – 'The Terror'.

NOVEMBER

18

1932 The Bodyline tourists dock at Fremantle, Western Australia.

1955 New South Wales (K. Miller 7–12) dismiss South Australia for 27, the lowest score in a Sheffield Shield match.

1985 Playing for Rajasthan, Pradeep Sunderam takes all ten Vidarbha wickets for 78 runs at Jodhpur, and sets a new Indian record with his match analysis of 16–154.

19

1841 Birth of Harry Jupp in Dorking. The Surrey batsman, notoriously difficult

Douglas Jardine with his MCC party for the 'bodyline' tour.

1956 CRICKETERS
A SERIES OF FIFTY

(1st SERIES, NUMBERS 1 to 25)

No. 10

P. R. UMRIGAR
(Gujerat and India)

A great all-rounder, P. R. Umrigar (born Bombay, 1926) is a medium-pace bowler and one of his country's best fielders. His height of over 6 feet and a series of mighty sixes which he scored during a West Indies tour led to his being dubbed the "palm tree hitter." He headed India's batting averages against Pakistan and has played in the Lancashire League as a professional.

Distributed by CBT LONDON W.2
ISSUED BY KANE PRODUCTS LTD.

1969 In his first innings in Test cricket G.R. Viswanath is caught Redpath, bowled Connolly for a duck at Kanpur. In the second innings he makes 137 to become the first Indian to score a century in his début match v Australia.

1970 Playing for South Australia v Western Australia at Perth, South African Barry Richards scores 325 in a day, going on to make 356 in a total of 372 minutes.

to get out, carries his bat through a completed innings 12 times. In the first-ever Test match he scores 63 and so is the first Englishman to reach a half-century in Test cricket.

1955 The Lal Bahadur Stadium, Hyderabad stages its first Test match, between India and New Zealand. In a drawn game Polly Umrigar scores 223 for India.

1976 India declare their first innings v New Zealand at Kanpur on 524–9. All their batsmen reach double figures but none scores a hundred in the highest Test total not to contain a century.

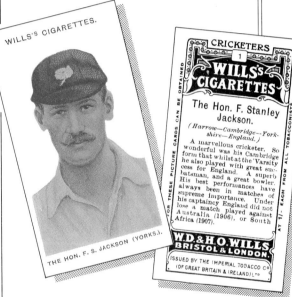

WILLS'S CIGARETTES.

THE HON. F. S. JACKSON (YORKS.).

CRICKETERS
1
WILLS'S CIGARETTES

The Hon. F. Stanley Jackson.

(*Harrow—Cambridge—Yorkshire—England.*)

A marvellous cricketer. So wonderful was his Cambridge form that whilst at the 'Varsity he also played with great success for England. A superb batsman, and a great bowler. His best performances have always been in matches of supreme importance. Under his captaincy England did not lose a match played against Australia (1905), or South Africa (1907).

W.D. & H.O. WILLS
BRISTOL & LONDON.

ISSUED BY THE IMPERIAL TOBACCO Co
(OF GREAT BRITAIN & IRELAND) L^td

FOR THESE PICTURE CARDS CAN BE OBTAINED — AT 1/- EACH FROM ALL TOBACCONISTS.

21

1870 Births of Hon. F.S. Jackson and Joe Darling. In 1905 they are opposing captains in the series between England and Australia.

1913 Jack Hobbs scores his 50th century with 170 for MCC v Eastern Province at Port Elizabeth – only 147 to go!

1938 MCC score 676 v Griqualand West at Kimberley, the highest total in South Africa. Hutton and Edrich share an opening stand of 263 and Paynter and Yardley also reach the century mark.

20

1912 Wilf Wooller is born. The Glamorgan captain and Welsh Rugby international is to become the leading opponent of Peter Hain's campaign against the South African tour of 1967. Birth of two players who go on to keep wicket for Cambridge University – S.P. Coverdale (1954) and C.F.E. Goldie (1960). Coverdale later joins Yorkshire and Goldie plays for Hampshire.

NOVEMBER

22

1943 Birth of Mushtaq Mohammad at Junagadh, Pakistan. He is one of the four Test-playing Mohammad brothers and the youngest of all Test cricketers.

1974 In the first Test to be played at Bangalore, between India and West Indies, two of the world's great batsmen make their débuts. Viv Richards launches himself quietly with scores of 4 and 3 and Gordon Greenidge hits 93 and 107. In the next Test Richards makes 192*.

1986 Sunil Gavaskar extends his Test record to 34 centuries with 176 v Sri Lanka at Kanpur.

23

1755 Birth of Thomas Lord at Thirsk, Yorkshire. The man after whom the world's most famous cricket ground is named, is brought up in Norfolk then moves to London and plays cricket for the White Conduit club. The first Lord's ground is opened at Dorset Square in 1787 and cricket is first played on the present ground in 1814.

1855 Birth of W.W. Read at Reigate. The Surrey batsman plays 18 times for England, hitting 117 v Australia at The Oval in 1884. Between 1873 and 1897 he hits 17,683 runs for his county at 32.80.

1858 Frank Hearne is born in Ealing. After playing for England in the first two Tests against South Africa under C. Aubrey Smith in 1889, he then represents South Africa in the third Test between the two countries in 1891.

24

1894 Birth of Herbert Sutcliffe near Harrogate. The great Yorkshire batsman scores 50,138 runs between 1919 and 1945, one of only seven men to pass the 50,000 landmark.

1930 Birth of Ken Barrington at Reading. A respected batsman and administrator, his untimely death in 1981 is a great loss to the game. In Test cricket he scores 6806 runs at 58.67.

1947 Natal wicket-keeper Billy Wade stumps seven Griqualand West batsmen in a Currie Cup match at Durban – a record for stumpings in Australia.

The ground near White Conduit House in 1787.

Another victim for Ian Botham as David Boon is trapped lbw.

Ken Barrington (back row, centre) with members of the Surrey 2nd XI in 1954. Also in the picture: Dave Halfyard (on Barrington's right), Roy Swetman (back row, extreme right) and Micky Stewart (seated, extreme right).

1955 Birth of Ian Botham at Heswall, Cheshire. The feats of the great Somerset, Worcestershire and England all-rounder appear under various dates in this book, most notably in the 1981 Test series v Australia.

NOVEMBER

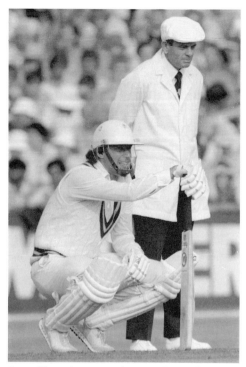

Imran Khan takes a rest at the non-striker's end.

25

1952   Birth of Imran Khan at Lahore. A cousin of Majid Khan, the Pakistan all-rounder and captain plays first-class cricket in England for Oxford University, Worcestershire and Sussex.

1980   Australian captain Greg Chappell hits 138* in the World Series match v New Zealand at Sydney. Len Pascoe takes 5–30 and Australia win by 94 runs.

1987   Abdul Qadir takes 9–56 in a day v England at Lahore.

26

1924   Birth of J.M. Patel. The Indian off-break bowler takes 9–69 v Australia at Kanpur in 1959–60, the fifth best haul in Test cricket and the best by an Indian.

1954   Colin Cowdrey makes the first of his record 114 appearances for England, v Australia at Brisbane. He makes 40 and 10, and England lose by an innings and 154 runs.

1959   Wally Grout makes eight dismissals v Pakistan at Lahore and Australia become the first side to win a series in that country.

27

1950   The first day of the match between Bombay Governor's XI and Commonwealth XI at Bombay marks the final day of first-class cricket for Raja Maharaj Singh. At the age of 72 he is the oldest first-class cricketer on record.

1970   Rodney Marsh (Australia) claims the first of his 355 Test victims, Geoffrey Boycott, on his début v England at Brisbane.

1981   Dennis Lillee (Australia) dismisses Wasim Raja (Pakistan) at Brisbane to record the fastest 300 wickets in Test cricket – 10 years 302 days. This record is later passed by Kapil Dev of India.

1983   Desmond Haynes (West Indies) is dismissed handled ball v India at Bombay after using a hand to deflect a ball from Kapil Dev away from his stumps.

28

1866   Birth of A.A. Lilley at Birmingham. The Warwickshire and England wicket-keeper takes 84 Australian victims in Test matches, the second highest by an England 'keeper after Alan Knott.

1919   Birth of Keith Miller in Victoria. One of Australia's great all-rounders, he scores 109 and takes 6–107 in one innings

20 years after his first Test, Bradman makes his final appearance at The Oval in 1948.

v West Indies at Kingston in 1954–55. In Tests he scores 2958 runs at 36.97 and takes 170 wickets at 22.97.

1975   Michael Holding makes his Test début v Australia at Brisbane.

29

1952   A last-wicket stand of 104 by Pakistanis Zulfiqar Ahmed (63*) and Amir Elahi (47) v India in Madras sends the total from 240–9 to 344 all out.

1963   Playing for Services v Northern Punjab at Amritsar, J.S. Rao takes two hat-tricks in an innings to become only the second man after Albert Trott (in 1907) to perform the feat.

1970   Colin Cowdrey surpasses Walter Hammond's Test record of 7,249 runs v Australia at Brisbane.

1984   Javed Miandad (103*) completes his second century of the match for Pakistan v New Zealand at Hyderabad, after making 104 in the first innings.

30

1857   Birth of Bobby Abel at Rotherhithe. The Surrey and England

batsman scores 357* v Somerset in 1899, and in his county career hits 27,605 runs at 36.61; with his slow deliveries he captures 256 wickets at 23.30.

1928   Don Bradman makes his Test début for Australia v England at Brisbane. He scores 16 and 1.

1969   Australian opener Bill Lawry carries his bat v India at Delhi, scoring a typically dogged 49 out of 107.

Bobby Abel, one of the great accumulators.

DECEMBER

1871 Birth of Archie (A.C.) MacLaren at Manchester. He still holds the record for the most runs scored in an innings in England, 424 for Lancashire v Somerset in 1895.

1901 Death of George Lohmann at Matjiesfontein, South Africa at the age of 36. The Surrey and England bowler, finest medium-pacer of his day, took 1841 first-class wickets at 13.73 and was good enough with the bat to hit three centuries.

1947 India are bowled out for 58 in their first official Test against Australia at Brisbane. E.R.H. Toshack takes 5–2 in 19 balls, the most economical 5-wicket figures in Test cricket.

2

1849 Birth of Francis Allan in Victoria. Selected for the first-ever Test v England in 1877, he goes off on a drinking spree and fails to reach the ground.

1932 First day of the Bodyline series, Australia v England at Sydney.

1956 Natal wicket-keeper Roland Pearce enjoys one of the most successful first-class débuts by a 'keeper. Against Western Province at Kingsmead, Durban he makes eight dismissals and scores 95, sharing in an opening stand of 163.

1977 After 12 players defect to Kerry Packer's WSC, Australia make wholesale changes for the Test v India at Brisbane, recalling Bobby Simpson as captain for his first Test in 10 years.

3

1890 W.E. Midwinter dies in Melbourne. The first man to take five wickets in an innings in the very first Test match, Midwinter represented Australia in that first series, but on England's third visit in 1881–82 he played for the tourists before returning to Australian colours the following year.

1905 Birth of Les (L.E.G.) Ames at Elham, Kent. He becomes the most prolific of wicket-keeper batsmen with more than 35,000 runs to his credit, scoring eight double centuries for Kent and 78 centuries.

1923 Birth of Trevor Bailey at Westcliff, Essex. He completes the 'double' eight times, and in his 61 Tests scores 2569 runs at 29.74 and takes 132 wickets at 29.21.

1931 Australia beat South Africa by an innings and 163 runs in the first Test to be played at the 'Gabba' in Brisbane.

4

1948 Playing for MCC v North Eastern Transvaal at Benoni, Denis Compton completes the fastest-ever triple century in 181 minutes with five sixes and 42 fours.

1950 On a 'sticky dog' at Brisbane, 20 wickets fall for 130 runs. In reply to Australia's 228, England reach 68–7 and declare (Bill Johnston 5–35). Australia then declare on 32–7 (Trevor Bailey 4–22, Alec Bedser 3–9), the lowest declared innings in Test cricket, and England stumble to 30–6 at close of play.

1964 In the most one-sided match of all time, Indian side Railways score 910–6 dec and dismiss Deva Ismail Khan for 32 and 27. The victory margin, an innings and 851 runs, is a world record.

1985 New Zealand beat Australia by six wickets in Perth to win the Tasman Trophy in its inaugural year.

DECEMBER

1928 England beat Australia by 675 runs at the Exhibition Ground, Brisbane. It is the first Test match at the ground, and England's winning margin is the biggest, by runs alone, in Test cricket.

1932 The Nawab of Pataudi snr makes his Test début for England, and like the two other cricketing princes from India – Ranjitsinhji and Duleepsinhji – he scores a century.

1964 Ken Barrington scores 142* for England v South Africa at Durban and becomes the first man to score a century against all the other Test-playing countries.

Graeme Pollock scoring a century for the Rest of the World against England in 1970.

1914 Birth of Cyril Washbrook at Barrow, near Blackburn. He makes his Lancashire début in 1933 and scores 34,101 runs at 42.67. In 1948 he receives a record benefit of £14,000 not surpassed until 1971. In Tests he is invariably linked with his opening partner Len Hutton (e.g. see 27th, below).

1949 Birth of Peter Willey at Sedgefield, Co. Durham. He plays for Northants 1966–83 then moves to Leicestershire. He makes his England début in 1976 and plays in 26 Tests until 1985.

1963 Graeme Pollock, South Africa's greatest Test batsman, makes his Test début v Australia at Brisbane. He scores 25.

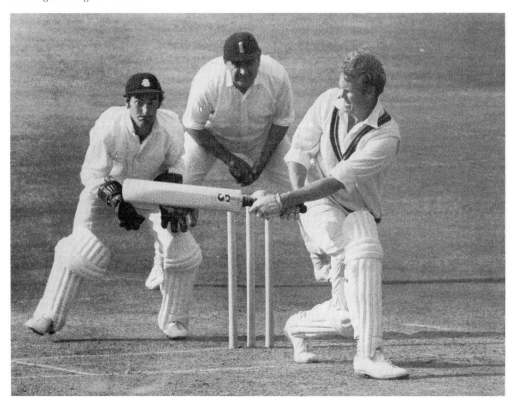

DECEMBER

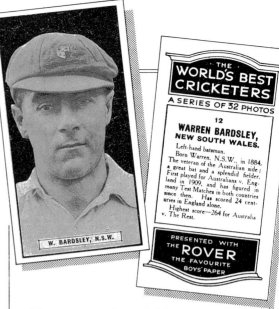

7

1882 Birth of Warren Bardsley. At The Oval in 1909 the Australian batsman becomes the first man to score a century in each innings of a Test match.

1978 South African Universities score 500–7 in the fourth innings to beat Western Province by three wickets.

1987 Aamer Malik makes his début for Pakistan v England at Faisalabad. On his first-class début, at the age of 17, he scores two centuries in the match, the youngest man to do so.

8

1927 R.J.O. Meyer, of Cambridge University and Somerset, takes 16–188 while playing for Europeans v Muslims at Bombay, then the best bowling figures in Indian first-class cricket.

1959 On the fourth day of the Test v Australia at Karachi, Pakistan score 104 runs, the second lowest total in a day's play. In the audience is the unfortunate President Eisenhower, the first US leader to watch a Test match.

1961 Against New Zealand at Durban, several great South African cricketers make their Test début – Peter Pollock, Eddie Barlow, Colin Bland, the world's best fielder, and M.K. Elgie, also a Scottish Rugby Union international.

9

1910 Australia score 494–6 on the first day of their first-ever Test v South Africa, at Sydney (Warren Bardsley 132, Clem Hill 191). It is the highest score made on the first day of any Test match.

1934 A.G. Chipperfield scores 99 for Australia on his Test début v England. He reaches 99* at lunch, then is caught behind off Ken Farnes on the third ball after the interval.

1958 During the first televised Test match in Australia, at Brisbane, Trevor Bailey takes 357 minutes to compile a half-century, the slowest in first-class history. He goes on to make 68 in 458 minutes.

10

1891 Thirty years after it was first formed, Yorkshire CCC is substantially reorganised to take on more or less its present form. Since then the club has won the Championship outright a record 29 times.

1958 In the Test at Brisbane (see above), Australia retaliate through J.W. Burke who takes 250 minutes to score 28*, batting through the innings as Australia reach the winning score of 147.

1983 Sunil Gavaskar gains the dubious distinction of becoming the first batsman to be dismissed by the first ball of a Test match for the second time when he is caught by Dujon off Marshall in India's 5th Test against the West Indies at Calcutta.

J.W. Burke (standing, extreme left) with the Australian team to visit England in 1956.

1954 Birth of Sylvester Clarke in Barbados. Like several other West Indians, he would have been a regular in any other international bowling line-up. Surrey and Transvaal benefit greatly from his availability.

1970 Play begins in the first Test match at the WACA (Western Australian Cricket Association). On a batsman's pitch Brian Luckhurst and John Edrich make centuries for England, and Ian Redpath and Greg Chappell do likewise for the hosts.

1982 Zaheer Abbas becomes the 20th player to score 100 centuries. Like Geoffrey Boycott he reaches the milestone during a Test match, playing for Pakistan v India at Lahore; he goes on to make 215.

Zaheer Abbas, several double centuries in his career.

DECEMBER

1919 Birth of Bhausahib Babasahib (B.B.) Nimbalkar at Bombay. He makes the third highest score in first-class history – 443* at Poona in 1948–49, and might have passed Bradman's then record of 452* but the opposition, Kathiawar, refuse to come out after the tea interval.

1959 Subhash Gupte takes 9–102 for India v West Indies at Kanpur. Then the best innings haul by an Indian bowler it is later beaten by J.M. Patel and Kapil Dev.

1977 Playing for Haryana v Jammu and Kashmir at Chandighar, slow left-armer Rajinder Goel produces the remarkable figures of 7–4 off 7 overs. His match return is 13–29.

1907 George Gunn is called into the England side at the last minute because of illness. He scores 119 in his début Test innings at Sydney and 74 in the second innings.

1965 Doug Walters also scores a début Test century on this day, hitting 155 v England at Brisbane.

1970 At Perth Greg Chappell emulates the feat with 108 v England.

1975 Also at Perth, Roy Fredericks scores a century for West Indies off 71 balls, then the fastest Test century in number of balls received.

14

1903 After scoring a century on his Test début for England, Reginald 'Tip' Foster goes on to score 287, the highest score in Test cricket until Andy Sandham's 325 in 1929–30.

1960 The first tie in Test cricket occurs at Brisbane at the end of the Australia v West Indies match. In the course of play Alan Davidson becomes the first player to complete a Test match double of 100 runs and 10 wickets, scoring 44 and 80 and taking 5–135 and 6–87.

1979 Dennis Lillee comes out to bat for Australia with a tin bat, but England captain Mike Brearley refuses to allow him to use it.

15

1894 S.E. Gregory completes his innings of 201 in the Test v England at Sydney, the first Test double century in Australia.

1933 India's oldest débutant takes the field v England at Bombay – R.J.D. Jamshedji, aged 41 years 27 days.

1977 Mudassar Nazar takes 9 hours 17 minutes to compile a century for Pakistan v England at Lahore, the longest Test century on record.

16

1882 Birth of Jack Hobbs at Cambridge. The greatest runmaker of all time, Hobbs in his Surrey and England career (1905–34) scores 61,237 runs. For his county he scores one triple century, 12 double centuries, 144 centuries.

1927 Don Bradman makes his first-class début for New South Wales v South Australia at Adelaide. He is aged 19 and scores 118.

1952 Birth of Joel Garner at Christchurch, Barbados. Standing 6ft 8in tall, he is one of the most feared bowlers of the 1980s, and in his 58 Tests takes 259 wickets at 20.97.

The Australia Cricket Club v. the England Cricket Club. on 14. 15. 17. 18 December 1894

Match Played at Sydney ... Result ...

1st Innings of Australia

BATSMAN.	RUNS SCORED.	HOW OUT.	BOWLER.	TOTAL.
Lyons		Bowled	Richardson	1
Trott H		Bowled	Richardson	12
Giffin G		caught Ford	Brockwell	161
Darling		Bowled	Richardson	0
Iredale F		caught Stoddart	Ford	81
Gregory S		caught Peel	Stoddart	201
Reedman		caught Ford	Peel	17
McLeod C		Bowled	Richardson	13
Turner		caught Gay	Richardson	1
Blackham		Bowled		74
Jones		Not out		11
UMPIRE	Byes 44			8
	Leg Byes ///			3
	Wide Balls /			1
	No Balls	Total of Innings.		586

Runs at the fall of each Wicket: 1 — 10 | 2 — 21 | 3 — 21 | 4 — 192 | 5 — 331 | 6 — 379 | 7 — 400 | 8 — 409 | 9 — 563 | 10 — 586

BOWLING ANALYSIS.

RUNS FROM EACH OVER.

BOWLER.		Overs	Maidens	Wides	No Balls	Runs	Wickets
Richardson		55.3	13			181	5
Peel		53	14			140	2
Briggs		25.4	4			96	—
Brockwell		22	7			78	1
Ford		11	2	1		47	1
Stoddart		3				31	1

Published by ALFRED SHAW & ARTHUR SHREWSBURY, Football and General Athletic Sports Warehouse, Carrington St. Bridge, Nottingham.

S.E. Gregory's record score at Sydney.

17

1927 Australian Bill Ponsford sets a new world record with his score of 437 for Victoria v Queensland at Melbourne. This beats his own world record, set five years earlier, by eight runs.

1954 Russell Endean (Transvaal) scores 197* before lunch v Orange Free State at Ellis Park, Johannesburg. This is the highest score in a pre-lunch session in first-class cricket.

1968 Brian Taber equals the world record, held by E. Pooley and D. Tallon, of 12 dismissals in a match by a 'keeper. Playing for New South Wales v South Australia at Adelaide, he holds nine catches and makes three stumpings.

DECEMBER

1900   Clem Hill scores 365* for South Australia v New South Wales at Adelaide, then the second highest innings after Archie MacLaren's 424.

1946   In the Australian innings of 659–8 dec v England at Sydney, wicket-keeper Godfrey Evans does not concede a single bye.

1960   Motganhalli Jaisimha, playing for India v Pakistan at Kanpur, scores 49 runs in a complete day's play, moving from 5* to 54*. This is the smallest number of runs scored by an individual in an uninterrupted day of Test cricket. He eventually reaches 99 and is run out going for a quick single; the whole innings lasts for 505 minutes.

1904   E.F. Waddy (129*) and W.P. Howell (128) complete a 9th wicket partnership of 221, playing for New South Wales v South Australia at Adelaide.

1924   Bill Ponsford (Australia) scores 110 on his Test début v England at Sydney.

1979   Geoffrey Boycott becomes the sixth man to carry his bat through an innings and finish on 99*. He performs the feat at Perth in a Test match; England are all out for 215.

1905   Birth of Bill ('Tiger') O'Reilly in New South Wales. The medium-paced leg-spinner takes 774 first-class wickets at 16.60, figures which support claims that he was the greatest ever bowler.

1948   England beat South Africa by two wickets at Durban in the only Test match to be won off the final ball. England's 9th wicket pair, Alec Bedser and Cliff Gladwin, need eight runs to win off the last eight-ball over. With one ball remaining the scores are level and they snatch victory off a leg-bye.

A memorable scoreboard at Adelaide.

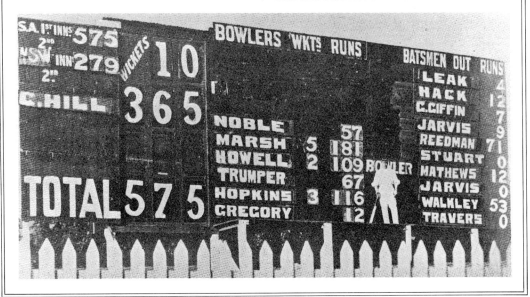

1959   Jasu Patel (India) seizes 9–69 when his off-spin takes eagerly to the newly laid turf at Kanpur and Australia are skittled out.

21

1934   Birth of Hanif Mohammad at Junagadh. In 55 Tests for Pakistan he scores 3915 runs at 43.98, with a best score of 337.

1945   Birth of Doug Walters at Dungog, New South Wales. After scoring a century v England on his Test début, he goes on to score 5357 Test runs at 48.26.

1977   Tony Mann (Australia) becomes the first nightwatchman to score a Test century, 105 v India at Perth, enabling Australia to win the match by two wickets.

22

1954   Frank ('Typhoon') Tyson makes his first impact on Australia's batsmen, taking 6–85 (10–130) and bringing England victory by 38 runs at Sydney.

1959   Border are dismissed for 16 in their first innings at East London and can reach only 18 in their second innings. Their combined total of 34 is the lowest for two completed innings in first-class cricket.

1962   Subhash Gupte dismisses 15 Vidarbha batsmen for 104 at Nagpur to return the best bowling figures in Indian first-class cricket.

Hanif Mohammad in 1959, the year of his record innings.

Bill O'Reilly, considered by many to be the greatest bowler of all-time.

DECEMBER

DECEMBER

23

1871 Death of Dr H.M. Grace, father of W.G., E.M. and G.F., at the age of 63.

1972 Bhagwhat Chandrasekhar takes 8–79 for India v England at Delhi but England win the match comfortably.

1981 Geoffrey Boycott passes Gary Sobers's record of 8032 Test runs, v India at Delhi, and finishes with an aggregate of 8114, later beaten by Sunil Gavaskar.

1982 Maninder Singh becomes India's youngest Test player when he makes his début v Pakistan at Karachi at 17 years 193 days.

24

1927 Walter Hammond makes his Test début, along with future Test captains Ian Peebles and R.E.S. Wyatt, v South Africa at Johannesburg. He makes 51 in his only innings and takes 5–36 in the second innings – a reminder of his all-round powers.

1932 Birth of Colin Cowdrey at Bangalore. Among his numerous feats for Kent and England he scores 307 for MCC v South Australia at Adelaide in 1962–63, the highest innings by an Englishman in Australia. In Test matches he scores 7624 runs at 44.06.

Dr H.M. Grace's three sons in the 1874 Gloucestershire side which played Yorkshire at Clifton College. W.G. is seated in the centre with G.F. on his left. E.M. is standing second from the right in the back row.

1938 Playing against South Africa at Johannesburg, Walter Hammond becomes the first player to score 6000 Test runs.

1938 Tom Goddard performs a Test hat-trick in Johannesburg, dismissing South African batsmen Nourse, Gordon and Wade.

2 5

Test cricket has been played on Christmas Day on the Indian sub-continent – though in England this and Boxing Day are more renowned for attempts to play charity matches in the worst imaginable conditions.

1891 Birth of Clarrie Grimmett at Dunedin, New Zealand. The leg-spinner later settles in Australia and becomes a universally feared opponent. Against Yorkshire at Sheffield in 1930 he takes 10–37. In his 37 Tests he takes 216 wickets for 24.21.

1956 Birth of Mansoor Akhtar in Pakistan. In 1976–77 he and Waheed Mirza put on a world record 1st-wicket stand of 561 for Karachi Whites v Quetta at Karachi.

1972 Tony Lewis, on his Test début, captains England to a six-wicket win over India in Delhi, contributing 70* in England's second innings.

2 6

1913 Wilfred Rhodes takes his 100th Test wicket v South Africa at the Old Wanderers ground, Johannesburg and becomes the first Englishman to complete the Test double of 1000 runs and 100 wickets.

1928 Alan Kippax and Hal Hooker complete a world record 10th-wicket partnership of 307 for New South Wales v Victoria at Melbourne.

2 7

1948 Len Hutton (158) and Cyril Washbrook (195) open the England innings v South Africa at Johannesburg with a stand of 359, made in 310 minutes.

1968 Garth McKenzie (Australia) takes 8–71 v West Indies at Melbourne.

1972 Ashley Mallett completes another eight-wicket haul for Australia – 8–59 v Pakistan at Adelaide.

1981 Playing against West Indies at Melbourne, Dennis Lillee takes the wicket of Larry Gomes, his 310th Test victim, a new world record beating that set five years earlier on the same ground by Lance Gibbs.

Caricature of Clarrie Grimmett in 1940 by Australian cartoonist Kerwin Maegraith.

DECEMBER

28

1926   Victoria complete their world-record innings of 1107, scored in two days in a Sheffield Shield match v New South Wales at Melbourne. One month later NSW gain partial revenge by dismissing Victoria for 35.

1975   Gary Cosier scores 109* on his Test début for Australia v West Indies at Melbourne, the first Australian to do so against West Indies.

1983   On reaching his century in the Madras Test v West Indies, Sunil Gavaskar passes Don Bradman's record of 29 Test match centuries.

29

1948   Eric Rowan, dropped by the South African selectors for the next Test, responds the following day by scoring 156* v England and saving the match for his country.

1952   Bert Sutcliffe completes his memorable 385 for Otago v Canterbury in a Plunket Shield match at Lancaster Park. This is the highest individual score in first-class cricket in New Zealand.

1983   Following his record-breaking century the previous day, Sunil Gavaskar goes on to score 236*, the highest score by an Indian in Test cricket.

30

1911   Sydney Barnes takes 4–1, reducing Australia to 11–4 on the first day of the Test at Melbourne. Exactly two years later he completes match figures v South Africa at Johannesburg of 8–56 and 9–103. These remain the best-ever Test figures until beaten by Jim Laker's 19–90.

1980   Multan, where Pakistan receive West Indies, becomes the 51st Test ground. It is a stormy baptism – an umpire arrives late on the first day, inflaming the crowd; at whom Sylvester Clarke later throws a brick; after which Alvin Kallicharran has to appeal to them on bended knees before some order is restored. A draw is the only possible outcome in such circumstances.

1982   England beat Australia at Melbourne by three runs, equalling the narrowest runs margin in Test history.

31

1954   Colin Cowdrey makes a superb 102 out of England's meagre total of 191 v Australia at Melbourne.

1980   Death of a grand old hitter, Arthur Wellard, at Sutton, Surrey aged 78. For Somerset he scores 11,462 runs, including only two centuries, but it was always by the way he scored them that he is remembered. So much so that people are apt to forget his bowling – 1517 first-class wickets at 24.32.

1981   Dennis Lillee finishes the year with a record bag of 85 Test wickets.

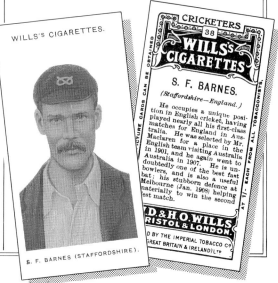

WILLS'S CIGARETTES.

CRICKETERS 38

WILLS'S CIGARETTES

S. F. BARNES.
(Staffordshire—England.)

He occupies a unique position in English cricket, having played nearly all his first-class matches for England in Australia. He was selected by Mr. Maclaren for a place in the English team visiting Australia in 1901, and he again went to Australia in 1907. He is undoubtedly one of the best fast bowlers, and is also a useful bat; his stubborn defence at Melbourne (Jan. 1908) helping materially to win the second Test match.

D.&H.O. WILLS
BRISTOL & LONDON.

D BY THE IMPERIAL TOBACCO Co
REAT BRITAIN & IRELAND) L^{TD}

S. F. BARNES (STAFFORDSHIRE).

Another big hit from Arthur Wellard in 1936.

ACKNOWLEDGEMENTS

All photographs used in this book are
from the archives of *The Cricketer*.
Cigarette cards, programmes and
scorecards are from the publisher's
private collection.

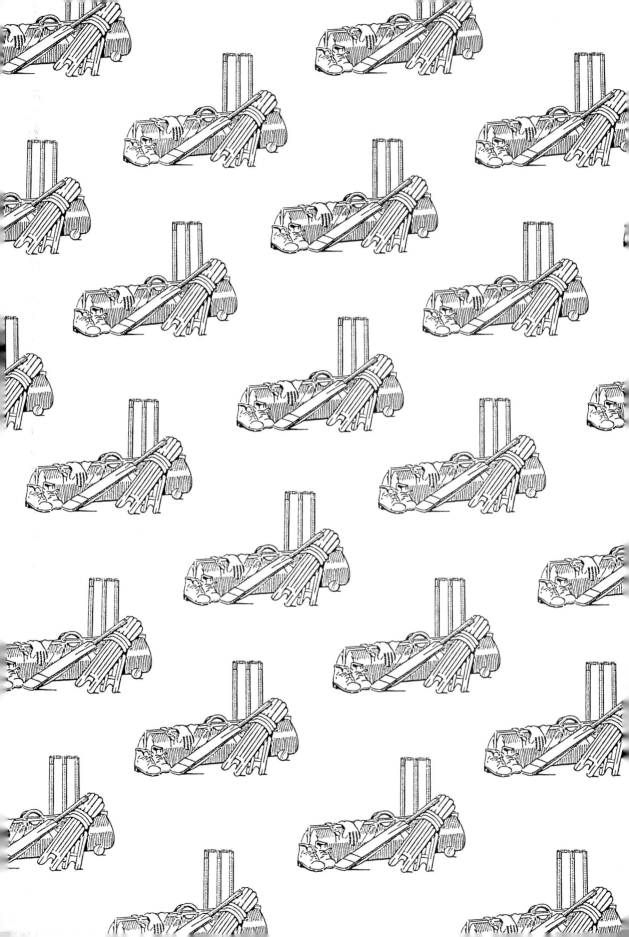

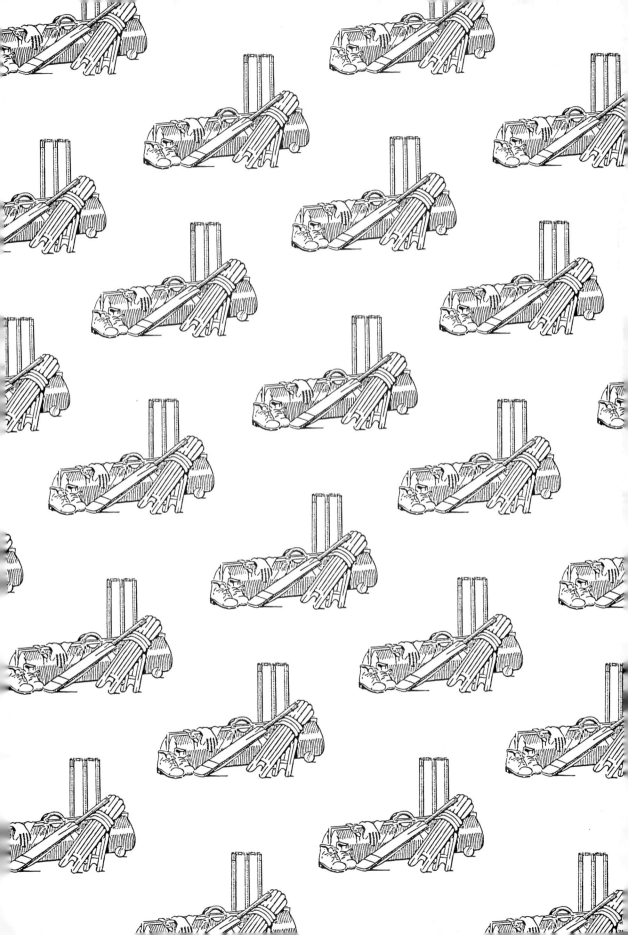